Joy Hunter

ALSO BY ALEXIS JONES

I Am That Girl

Machu Picchu brought a spiritual awakening that included one of the best make-outs and worst hangovers of my life. I learned about the ugly reality of sex trafficking and the delicious food in Thailand, art and dirty dancing as acceptable forms of rebellion in Cuba, and that you can drink all the wine and eat all the bread you want and for some mysterious reason you won't gain weight in Italy. I learned about racial inequity and the absurdity of shark cage diving when I got so scared, I peed in my wet suit at least three times in Cape Town. I also learned that Tokyo is the gold standard for sushi, selfies, and public transportation, and that I'm capable of breaking a human hand, which I'm pretty certain I did on an overnight train in China when a guy tried to feel me up, thinking I was asleep.

Forty-nine American states, fifty-two countries, seven continents, lots of stomach bugs, head lice, make-outs, carbs, and a broken hand later, I am a tapestry of the sights, sounds, smells, tastes, feelings, people, and stories I have collected during my travels. And each person I have come across exists somewhere inside of me so that I have a name and a face for every time someone references a group of people they can't relate to or understand. Proximity is the gateway to empathy, and I had it in spades.

In addition to providing a window into different cultures and worlds, chasing adventures around the globe also offered me a welcomed and relaxed counterbalance to my gold star–seeking, productivity-obsessive, manically structured life back home. Somehow these adventures temporarily silenced the chaos inside of me and lulled to sleep my inner dragon, the part of me that anxiously wanted to control every outcome and sought approval from everyone.

I was drowning in the pressure others had placed on me—or more accurately, that I had placed on myself. My addiction to hunting adventures in foreign lands became the only way I knew how to turn the dial of my joy up louder than the deafening sounds of my anxiety, my impossible expectations, and my feelings of unworthiness. When I was away from "life" and traveling, I was able to be present; more importantly, it was only then that I was able to feel a simplicity and calmness that otherwise eluded me.

So, by the time I was in my early twenties, there had become two of me, bifurcated between obligation and joy. I was my dutiful self, checking off boxes, people pleasing, and suppressing what was in my gut, until a metaphorical low-gas light would go on and I'd be at a crawling speed until "empty" began flashing in bright red. Then I'd book another trip to a destination where I would be among fellow seekers, hiking perilous mountains, skinny-dipping in ice cold streams, or curling up next to warm campfires. My energy—depleted by expectations, opinions, the judgment of others—would eventually refind its brilliance, and I would return to "real life," once again with a full tank of gas.

What I didn't know then, though, was that my real life could be as glorious and vibrant as the foreign lands in which I'd been seeking refuge. I didn't know then that the most profound and exhilarating pilgrimage of my life would not be to a far-off land, or to a wilderness on the remotest edge of the globe, but instead, within my very own heart and mind. After a month-long road

Joy Hunter

MESSY FACEPLANTS, RADICAL LOVE, AND THE JOURNEY THAT CHANGED EVERYTHING

ALEXIS JONES

HARMONY

NEW YORK

harmonybooks.com

Harmony Books is a registered trademark, and the Circle colophon
is a trademark of Penguin Random House LLC.

Library of Congress Cataloging-in-Publication Data
is on file with the publisher.

ISBN: 978-0-5935-7806-3
Ebook ISBN: 978-0-5935-7807-0

Printed in the United States of America

Book design by Andrea Lau
Jacket design by Caroline Johnson
Jacket photographs by Seth K. Hughes / Image Source / Getty Images (landscape),
owngarden / Moment / Getty Images (clouds)
Photograph on pages ii and iii by Rob Bates Photography / Shutterstock

10 9 8 7 6 5 4 3 2 1

First Edition

For Bradley, the greatest love of my life.
I still have to pinch myself that I get to do life with you.

AUTHOR'S NOTE

Each of us has a brilliant, messy, troubling, wild, weird, and specific story to tell. It's daunting to cherry-pick which experiences are the most defining, the most relevant, without succumbing to too much navel gazing. The emotional and literal journey I chronicle here reflects a sharp turn off the expected and demanding road I'd been driving down most of my life. I'd like to think that this departure will be one of the most significant landmarks of my life, and as a result, worthy of sharing with others.

I've tried to tell my story in a straight line, but life never unfolds that neatly. So, in a few places, I've conflated moments and summarized conversations for purposes of clarity. In most cases, I've used real names. But in a few cases, I've changed names and/or potentially identifying characteristics so that the person in question might retain their privacy and be shielded from scrutiny.

Oh, one more thing. I originally wanted to call this book *The Lucky Girl Who Got Everything She Ever Thought She Wanted, But Only*

Found Joy After Faceplanting in Lots of Shit—A Memoir. My publisher pointed out that as a practical matter, this was a bit of a mouthful and would be hard to fit on the cover. She also gently suggested that it might lack a certain inviting tone and might be a little off-putting to readers. I got the point, but *Joy Hunter* still embraces and reflects on all of the sentiments of the lengthier title. I *do know* how charmed my life has been in so many ways. But for what it's worth, my suggestion *is* pretty darn accurate.

PROLOGUE

At the fifty-year reunion of my high school's founding and my own twenty-year reunion, the principal presented the first "Distinguished Alumni" awards and I was a recipient (along with NFL QB and Super Bowl Champion Drew Brees, who graduated five years before me). A lifelong journaler, I riffled through dozens of dusty journals, looking for acceptance speech inspiration. In one that properly crystalized my teenage glory days, I found this entry and I included it in my speech.

> "Dear Lex, I hope you are everything and more than the dreams you have right now. I hope you're not so focused on the plan you have for your life that you don't allow yourself to be surprised, I hope that when you fall you have the guts to get back up—not once but every single time. I hope that when you get your heart broken because people keep saying heartbreak is inevitable, that you'll choose to love again.

People also say no matter what in life, that you'll have problems so I hope you sign up to solve big, huge, massive ones, the kind that would scare other people but excite you. More than anything, I hope in the midst of your crazy and awesome life that you pause along the way— because while I'm sure you'll be a fine adult and have some badass job doing good things and saving the world, I want you to remember that your heartbeat matters more than all the noise trying to drown out the preciousness of the here and now . . . because this moment right now is all we ever have.

And I know you, so don't climb so high and run so fast that you forget to look around and soak everything up because before you know it you're going to blink and be an adult who forgets how to play and laugh and dance and dream. I just see so many adults who have lost their spark and I don't want that for you. I guess what I'm saying is I just don't want you to forget me when you grow up, because I am your spark.

So just promise me that you won't lose me or snuff me out. Promise me that you'll always rage and burn and you'll be more than just a spark, I want you to promise me that you'll be a motherfucking bonfire. Also, I know this is random, but I do hope Jimmy Hamilton says yes when you ask him out to prom, but that is neither here nor there."

I went on to say to the audience:

I think teenager Lex was at times wiser than me now . . . but may we all follow her lead in making time to be present to the here and now. And may we be brave enough to relight our spark if it has gone out, or add more logs to our fire if it's gone cold and may our bonfire rage on, so we never forget the punk kid inside each of us that knew exactly who they were before the world got its hands on us . . . for we owe it to them and no one else . . . to remember our inherent greatness.

In the late spring of 2020, my husband, Brad, our best friend, Luke, and I embarked on a road trip around the great American West in an attempt to relight our respective sparks. We did it because we could—the pandemic had effectively paused my work as an activist and motivational speaker, and it allowed Brad and Luke to work remotely. But mostly we did it because we *had* to. The three of us—though for different reasons—were all profoundly heartbroken. This trip was something we could hold on to, something we could *do*, something to look forward to. We decided to leave behind the place that reminded each of us of what we had lost and to venture forth in the hopes of discovering what might still lie ahead, both inside ourselves and each other. In agreeing to go on the road trip, I was signing up for all of the things I'd spent a lifetime avoiding.

I was saying YES to uncertainty;

YES to the unknown;

and YES to the uncontrollable.

Joy Hunter

CHAPTER ONE

Summer camp and traveling have always been in my blood. At the age of seven, I first left home and headed to Laity Lodge Youth Camp (LLYC) for two unfailingly fantastic weeks. Even now as I type, I can't wipe the smile off my face because I LIVED FOR SUMMER CAMP. I'm using shouty caps because that's the best way I know to explain the energy surging through my body as I think about my happy place. For fourteen consecutive summers, the memories I made in the sweltering Texas hill country—sleeping in un-air-conditioned hot boxes each night—remain some of the best experiences of my life.

LLYC was a coed Christian sports camp, and we filled our days there with every team sport imaginable, plus arts and crafts, rappelling, archery, riflery, horseback riding, and mountain biking. At night we watched movies on the tennis courts and caught lightning bugs in the palms of our soft adolescent hands. I'm pretty sure I didn't end a session without a bona fide camp boyfriend, but we were careful to make sure that when we were slow dancing, there was always enough room between us for Jesus.

When I look at old photos from these summers, tucked away in a metal lunch box in my closet, I see our sun-kissed faces and tan lines and am reminded of melting s'mores, frozen Snicker bars, dancing under the stars, food fights, and swimming in the emerald green water of the river that ran like a snake through the carved out canyon walls. From the moment I arrived at camp until the moment I departed, I wasn't just happy; it felt as if my heart was so full that whatever liquid joy had been pumped into me was spilling out all over me and around me, coating everything it touched, myself included, in a warm, gooey metallic gold. This pure, unadulterated joy was my default setting at camp. Back then, I didn't have to try to find it or discover it. It felt as natural as breathing.

As I grew older, I discovered that traveling, especially to unknown places, offered me this same kind of joy. When I was fifteen, I traveled outside of the country for the first time, flying to Costa Rica to live with my brother and his family for the summer. At first, the foreignness intimidated me; I was afraid to venture out into this new, unknown world. It felt safe inside the little house with the familiar faces of my sister-in-law and my toddler-aged niece and nephew. But after a few days of tagging along with them while my brother worked, I realized that I would likely die from boredom if I spent an entire summer inside.

My first foray out was to the convenience store on the corner of our block. In carefully studied Spanish, I asked to buy a candy bar. The next day I made it a block farther. And a little farther the day after that, quickly walking back to the safety of home base after each outing. I began to recognize the neighbors and got to know the neighborhood, eventually daring to use my budding vocabulary and imperfectly conjugated verbs as I waved and walked on by. At sixteen years old, I returned home at the end of the summer having experienced my first adult beverage, my first night of stoned laughter, and my first nightclub dance party. I also returned with an earned sense of confidence, an insatiable desire to keep exploring, and a permanent tattoo that I effectively hid from my dad . . . for years.

It's as if the universe heard my beacon going off like a Bat-Signal and sent me a fairy god/grandfather a year later who would support my newfound itch to travel despite my family's modest income (a euphemism for my family just being perpetually broke). Having inherited all of his financial wealth, Mr. Dunn was like a surrogate father to my mom and a surrogate grandfather to me. As he was well into his eighties, his passion for travel had become too difficult for him to pursue alone. He was estranged from his only relative—a son—so during all my high school holidays, my mom and I were invited to join him on all his extraordinary adventures around the world, at the tail end of his beautiful life. In return for his outrageous generosity, and being the effective "help," we earned our keep, overseeing all the travel logistics, pushing his wheelchair, and keeping him amused with our fresh-eyed views of the world we were exploring together. Like a twenty-first-century Cinderella, I was swept away to magical places we could never have otherwise afforded: Morocco, Portugal, Italy, Greece, Monaco, France, Switzerland,

Spain, and the Channel Islands. Then when the proverbial clock turned midnight, my mom and I would humbly return to our tiny rented home in Cuernavaca, and I'd pray our phone wasn't turned off again because we couldn't pay the bill that month. When Mr. Dunn passed away a few years later, he left his fortune to his son, but he left me forever richer in life experience and perspective, because he opened my mind to just how big and beautiful the world was outside of my hometown. He also left me bitten by an insatiable travel bug.

As a broke college kid, I would save up every cent I could to buy the cheapest tickets I could find to get to yet another far-away, off-the-beaten-path land. Often traveling alone, I'd stay in youth hostels and eat street food to accommodate my shoestring budget, which also came with countless bouts of some version of Montezuma's revenge, one life-threatening round of E. coli, and a mutant strain of lice that took me three months to cure. I learned more about myself and the world with no more than a backpack and a deep reverence for the people generously hosting me in whatever country I found myself exploring.

Over the next two decades, travel would provide me with the greatest education of all. I thought I knew a thing or two about growing up as a poor kid from "the other side of the tracks," but the landfill slums of Cambodia and the destitution rampant in the rural outskirts of India gave me a whole new perspective on the relativity of wealth. In Istanbul, I learned that religious inclusivity was possible and haggling in the Grand Bazaar was an official sport. Antarctica stoked a fire in me for environmental stewardship and instilled an absolute obsession with penguins.

trip, chasing adventures and searching for joy, I would discover a life where I didn't have to warrior all the time: striving, proving, impressing, or achieving. That my real life could reflect that same divine place of surrender I always accessed on my unconventional adventures abroad. The open American road would teach me that like Dorothy on her yellow brick road adventures, all the power I was attempting to accrue externally had ironically been inside me all along.

CHAPTER TWO

I've kept a journal ever since elementary school. My first one was pastel colored with a magnificent white unicorn on the cover and a tiny golden lock that promised to protect all of my childhood secrets, especially the names of my brothers' best friends, many of whom I had crushes on.

When I was certain no one was around, I would curl up on my bed, carefully unlock the journal, and proceed to record all my hopes and dreams, fears and doubts, assuming that by writing them down, I might sway the universe in the unfolding of my life.

I recently sat down and looked through three decades of these chronicles and I noticed that there was a single consistent thought that I'd written numerous times, the first time while in third grade.

"I know I'm being lied to. I just don't know about what, exactly . . ."

Mount Whitney is the highest point in the continental US at 14,505 feet. Death Valley is the lowest point in the United States, clocking in at 282 feet below sea level. I know this because the most extreme, demanding endurance race on the planet—the Badwater 135—covers the 135 miles from Death Valley to Mount Whitney, the lowest to the highest points in America. And for years, I have daydreamed about one day training and running it. My life would eventually feel like this race in reverse; falling from the summit of my mountain, not just to the bottom, but what would eventually become below sea level. "I'm sorry to inform you that the information you provided for your biological father is incorrect" were the sixteen words—said aloud on speakerphone—that started this free fall. They took my breath away; they cracked the foundation of my world.

I was in an Uber heading to the airport, having just left West Point, where I had spoken to a group of cadets as part of an initiative by ProtectHer, a company I had started to inspire and educate young men on the importance of protecting and respecting women. The talk had gone well, but now, almost a decade and a half after my first public speech, I was running on fumes. I was on the road 250-plus days a year for work. I just kept saying yes. Yes to more gigs, yes to more travel, yes to more money, yes to more press, yes to more accolades, yes to more awards.

Truthfully, my "check engine" light had been on for years, but I still refused to slow down. Being determined and scrappy was all I ever knew. Growing up, I was the baby girl, flanked by four big brothers. It was family tradition for the boys to routinely challenge one another to some version of king of the hill. Entirely uninvited, I'd throw myself into the wrestling mayhem and within minutes find myself squished at the bottom of the pile. I'd somehow crawl my way out, only to fling myself back into the mosh pit of adolescent male sweat, jockeying for some kind of toughness pecking order.

Once, my six-foot-seven brother accidentally kicked me in the face, although it was more likely that I face-butted his foot. The gushing blood didn't upset me as much as it fired me up to continue to go after him. "Oh shit, I'm so sorry!!" he yelled as I chased him down, even more hell-bent on wrestling, blood and all.

I would go on to become the defiant girl who'd sneak into her brother's room to steal his Teenage Mutant Ninja Turtle underwear, wearing them with secret pride under her white lacy Easter dress. The girl who wore her baseball cap turned backward to hide a long ponytail in a field full of boys. I'd ceremoniously point my bat to the outfield, spitting sunflower seeds from the stash of them stored in my cheek, daring the pitcher to throw a pitch he thought I couldn't hit. With an entourage of big brothers sitting in the stands rooting for me, I knew they too expected me to Babe Ruth it over the fence. Looking back, I had adopted a toughness I can now see was deeply steeped in masculine stoicism: no tears, no fear, no emotions, no vulnerability, no asking for help and certainly no slowing down. Ever.

When I wasn't practicing becoming an MMA fighter or

baseball player, I could usually be found curled up reading comic books. I'd lay back with my hand behind my head and my legs crossed, daydreaming about being chosen for some extraordinary purpose, wondering about what kind of superpower might be revealed in the years to come.

These days I was all tapped out when it came to any kind of superpower. I was unrecognizable from the energetic and rebellious girl I had been. As I sat in the backseat of the Uber trying to navigate my way through what would be a life-changing call, my body was protesting against countless red-eye flights and my refusal to leave time between speaking events to properly rest and recharge. I was in chronic physical pain, but I had also grown accustomed to feeling existentially exhausted. Today in particular, I was operating on less than three hours of sleep and too much coffee.

Weeks before, I'd agreed to be featured on a television show that partnered with Ancestry.com as publicity for a speaking tour I was invited to with two of my sheroes, Glennon Doyle and Abbey Wambach. I had provided the producers with a saliva sample and as much information about my relatives as I could. The concept of the show was that the host would then walk me through the results of the test, revealing various facts about my family history. I was deeply interested to learn more about my lineage; up until that point I had only an outline understanding of it, but much of the detail was blurry at best.

I did know that my father came from a line of well-to-do Texans. His father was a state legislator and a prominent judge in Austin. My grandma Bess was a highly respected, proud, God-fearing pistol of a woman. They had both been dear friends with President LBJ and Lady Bird Johnson. They were political royalty and looked like a movie star couple.

I have a special place in my heart for Bess. She made up for her diminutive, five-foot stature with the number of damns she gave and the height of her hair that brought her ever so slightly closer to God. Whether it was the treatment of the disabled, equal access to education, homelessness, women's rights, or any other group she felt like society had overlooked, she made them her business, long before it was considered cool to repost woke hashtags on social media.

My grandmother impressed upon me the fact that often people claiming to be Christian don't act very Christ-like. She always preferred the colorful version of Jesus—an inclusive, rebellious, radically loving justice warrior. She followed his lead to the letter. She challenged power structures that only benefited the few who looked like her, leveraging and sacrificing her own privilege and comfort to advocate for the unseen and undervalued. Someone at church once pulled me aside and said, "You know, your grandmother singlehandedly determined who ran for office in the state's capital and, more importantly, who won." It was true. Bess Jones was a kingmaker during a time when her being the rightful queen was simply denied by the power-wielding good ole boys of Texas. Like so many women of her generation, she was a pacing lion, caged by a patriarch that undoubtedly and rightfully feared her.

"Always seek to leave things, places, and people better than you found them," she'd say as she brushed my long hair. "Women my age didn't have the opportunities you have today, and we fought like hell to make sure you have the choices that we didn't. But know that along with opportunities come responsibilities. You're going to change the world, Alexis. I know it," she'd say in a rebellious whisper.

"So, make sure to give 'em the horns and never, ever stop fighting. Trust me, they are more scared of you than you should ever be of them," she'd say as she cracked a knowing smile. Looking back, it's as if she were training me to become the warrior she always knew herself to be. Honestly, I was certain not even God would get the last say with her.

My mom—Claudia—had a more *colorful* family. She was dealt a lethal combination of generational poverty, generational lack of education, generational abuse, and generational incest, all circling her crib like vultures. No one from her family had graduated from high school, much less college. Claudia grew up fast and she grew up hard, having been molested by her stepfather at a very young age. She got pregnant at sixteen, with my oldest brother, Scott. Out of obligation, she ended up marrying her baby daddy boyfriend, which came as no surprise given her upbringing.

As a little girl, my mom was bathed in a very different version of God. She sat in a church pew for hours each Sunday watching her fundamentalist preacher grandfather get all kinds of worked up—red-faced and spitting as a form of exclamation. Her grandpa always managed to weave in some catastrophic hellfire and brimstone consequences to what always felt to her like humans doing rather ordinary human things. Sex was at the top of the "naughty/don't do" list. She joked that out of shame alone, she married just about every guy she ever slept with. Apparently, all that preaching wasn't very effective for my mom or her mom—my Grandma Pat—who was married nine times, five times to the same man.

Pat endured nine full-term pregnancies and lost five of the babies shortly after birth, which resulted in a long stay at a mental hospital—complete with electric shock therapy—to treat the sadness and anger that came with those losses. That institutionalized "help" left her sometimes unable to recognize her living children.

Despite her rough start, my mother managed to end the cycles of abuse for my four brothers and me. She worked two jobs and put all five of us through undergraduate, graduate, and/or law school. When I was eight years old, I cheered alongside my brothers as she walked the stage, celebrating her *own* college graduation.

Needless to say, my mom is a fucking warrior.

She is my best friend and the sun around which the rest of our family orbits. She is the matriarch in every sense of the word. A juggernaut of grit, faith, and resilience. Never once has she made an excuse for the crappy cards she was dealt. Instead, she chose to play the shit out of them.

So, I felt I knew everything I needed to know about my mom already. I was decidedly less eager to learn about the hellish fires that had forged the phoenix she had become.

Checking my voicemail from the back of the Uber, I'd

received an urgent message that someone named Jennifer from Ancestry needed to speak to me to explain that they would need to cancel the segment I was supposed to be doing for them. My guess was that Ancestry had booked a bigger "name" for their show and they wanted to break that uncomfortable news in private. I called back, putting the phone on speaker. Jennifer was perky and perfectly pleasant when she answered. But then she got serious. "I guess I'll just dive right in," she said. "The thing is, Alexis, I really love my job . . . and moments like this make it really hard." Her obvious discomfort made my palms feel scratchy, so I politely tried to give her an out.

"It's okay, I understand you had to go in another direction. It's all good. I don't take this kind of stuff personally."

"Another direction? Oh, well that's not it at all," she said. Her voice had become low; perky had officially left the building.

My silence confirmed what had to be her fear: I was completely in the dark. To her credit, she didn't beat around the bush any further. "I'm sorry to inform you, but the information you provided for your biological father is incorrect." There they were: the sixteen damning words.

My eyes grew wide and I held the phone away from my face as if staring at the screen would help me understand what this stranger was trying to communicate. I asked her to repeat what she'd just said. She did, this time wrapping the news in a softer, velvety tone of voice to cushion the knock-out blow she was delivering.

I sat there silently as my mind tried to process her statement: that the man I had known all my life, my daddy, my real-life superhero who tucked me in at night, who coached everything I had ever played, who kissed me on my head, called me his "greatest treasure," and walked me down the aisle . . . was *not* my biological father? Surely this was some kind of clerical error.

I suddenly realized I was holding my breath and clenching every aching muscle in my body. Like a wounded dog, I nipped at the hand of the person trying to clean the cut. I'm pretty sure I called Jennifer *professionally irresponsible* and *reckless* and used a few other choice words about the integrity of her company, as if insulting her would miraculously make everything she'd said untrue. Ever professional, however, Jennifer said she understood my reaction. "This is big news," she said. "You may want to talk to your mother."

Boy, did I ever. I knew my mom would share my outrage and confirm Ancestry's egregious mistake.

I hung up on Jennifer, fingers shaking as I navigated my phone, and dialed my mom's cell. When she picked up, I launched breathlessly into what I was sure she'd agree was an outrageous faux pas.

"Mom, there is this woman, her name is Jennifer, she works at Ancestry.com. Remember I'm supposed to do that TV show segment?"

I didn't wait for her to respond. I was frenetic, panicked, desperate.

"She's clearly mistaken. She doesn't know anything about me, and she's messed up my whole taping, which is supposed to happen tomorrow."

"Whoa, whoa, slow down. I don't know what you're talking about, honey," she said with sincere concern.

I pressed on petulantly. "Mom, she said Dad isn't my biological father, which is absurd because obviously he is and she's wrong and she's going to be in big trouble when they sort this out because I told her it was professionally reckless and . . ."

As I went on and on, recapping the conversation, all I heard on the other end of the line was silence.

"Mom? Momma? Did I lose you? Did you hear what I said?"

Uncharacteristically quietly, she finally spoke up. "Ummm . . . well . . . Yes, I'm here. . . . It's just that . . . Uhhh . . ." I could hear her gasping for deep breaths as she attempted to find words.

In the midst of her neither denial nor confirmation, I felt like I had been struck by lightning. I immediately understood that my mom knew *exactly* what I was talking about. The electricity now surging through my body confirmed beyond a shadow of a doubt that what had been revealed to me was in fact true. I knew that Pandora's box wasn't just open but that the box was turned upside down, its secret contents now on full display. I immediately hung up and turned off my phone, knowing she'd be calling back.

And then stored memories of curious childhood incidents flashed across my mind.

Like the time I'd come home from school asking questions about dominant and recessive genes because we were learning in seventh-grade science how they worked. How was it, I asked my mom, that I had brown eyes (a dominant gene) if hers were green (a recessive gene) and Daddy's eyes were blue (also a recessive gene)? My mother's response was prickly and disproportionate, as though I'd touched the edge of an electric fence: "I don't know how, but you can!" she yelped. "Now, go finish cleaning your room!" This registered as strange to me not because of the science but because my room was always clean, and I knew she knew that.

Like the time I asked where the "moon shape" of my eyes came from and why I was so much "tanner" than my siblings, each time inching too close to that electric fence. My mom quickly shrugged off my questions, referencing some distant Native American relative on her dad's side of the family.

Like the fact that our fourth-grade teacher always confused me and my best friend, Elena Garcia, a half-white, half-Latina girl who everyone said looked like my twin despite both my parents clearly being Caucasian.

I stared out the window of the car and tried not to link these memories. Individually, all of them seemed harmless—inconclusive even—but strung together, they seemed to whisper a dangerously different narrative from the story I had been told and was now getting paid to tell for a living.

Suddenly, I became painfully aware that my Uber driver had just witnessed this entire, incredibly personal conversation on speaker. I held back fiery tears and thought maybe if I just didn't say anything, he would pretend with me that the call hadn't been horrifying. That I was fine. That everything was fine. That I wasn't a girl having a total identity crisis in the back of his car.

But he was too kind for that act. He adjusted his rearview mirror to catch my eye.

"Ma'am. Holy shit. Are you okay? I mean, that was some heavy shit. Girl, you need a hug? I can pull over."

I didn't dare look up into his sympathetic eyes. I continued to stare at my clenched hands.

"Well okay, I'm here," he continued before trailing off. "I'd need a hug if I were you, but whatever you need. I'm here."

It was the kindness of this stranger that put me over the edge. I buried my face in my hands and the tears I had been fighting back burst forth. I managed to ask his name through my sobs, and he told me it was Jerome.

"Well thank you, Jerome," I squawked. "Your hug offer means more than you know."

"I meant it, ma'am," he said kindly, and then let me be with my thoughts as he ferried me one step closer to my hometown and the conversation I would have to continue with my mother once I got there. I was utterly terrified to even consider how this might affect my relationship with my dad.

———

My mom has always been both a dazzling mystery and a walking juxtaposition: strength and vulnerably, brilliance and messiness, charisma and insecurity, grace and ferocity. She was a piece of coal that had endured the pressures of a hard life so well that she emerged as a raw, brilliant diamond, even if she had more rough patches than smooth. For as long as I can remember, my mom was, and still is, the center of my universe. Not *part* of my story, but my *entire* story.

My dad had heard about my mom before he ever met her. She was a legend. A much-talked-about beauty who worked at the local dive bar. My dad went in to see what all the fuss was about. "Sure enough, it was true," he told me. "Your mom wasn't just the most beautiful woman I'd ever seen, she turned out to also be the smartest person I'd ever met." I think he liked emphasizing the importance of brains *and* beauty for me, since girls were usually expected to choose between them.

When she met my dad, my mom already had two sons from two previous marriages. She carried with her the weight of the shame she associated with the perceived failure of her divorces. So, when she met Mark Jones, tied the knot, and had three more children, it felt like a tiny bit of redemption from her losing marriage record. Third time's the charm (*insert winky face here*). Well, until that marriage ended as well.

My dad always provided the necessary structure in the lives of his kids—not just for his own three, but all *five* of Mom's kids—and my mother always respected him for that. My mom has a wild spirit and thrives on novelty, excitement, and adventure. My dad prefers comfort and consistency, sitting in the same chair, watching sports, and musing over his ever-growing coin collection. She is a bird who has wanted to circle the globe a thousand times. He is a fish that prefers his bowl to an ocean. After seven years of marriage, they surrendered to the fact that their relationship was never going to be sustainable, and so they ended it. In the multiple-marriage department, the apple (my mom) didn't fall from the tree (Grandma Pat). My dad ended up being my mom's third husband; eventually she would have five.

But as wild and carefree as she is, my mother has an unfathomable work ethic. She expected the same kind of hard work from her children. When I was six—as a way to make extra money—my brothers and I helped Mom clean a local bar seven mornings a week. By first grade, I was cleaning urinals, vacuuming up cigarette butts, and stocking beer before most of my friends' alarm clocks had gone off. My mom was paid in cash. I was paid in Dorito chips and Dr. Pepper. My friends would casually reference their maids assuming I could relate, not knowing I was one myself.

A single parent with five kids, my mom worked two jobs and went to night school throughout much of my childhood, easily clocking eighty-plus–hour weeks. She worked as a paralegal during the day, leaving the house every morning dressed in some kind of stiff, dark skirt-suit, wearing the only pair of reasonable high heels she owned. She always twisted her long, thick, mermaid-like hair into a professionally appropriate bun that required about a hundred bobby pins. I'd stare in awe at her as she plucked pins from her pursed lips, each one quickly disappearing into her mane, as we both stared at her reflection in the bathroom mirror.

When home from her day job, my mom would quickly

change into a T-shirt and loose-fitting jeans and allow her dark, thick locks to spill down her back. She'd make our Hamburger Helper dinner barefoot, singing and swaying along to Garth Brooks, and smiling at me as she sipped a cold beer. I'd sing along, mesmerized; I worshipped her.

For the next couple of hours, my mom was a blur. She'd do loads of laundry, make the rounds to ensure that we were doing our homework, get us ready for bed. And then another wardrobe transformation and she'd head out to her bartending job at a local spot called Deep Eddy. In the mornings, the stale smell of her customers' cigarette smoke still lingered in her hair. The nights she wasn't serving beer, she was determined to complete an undergraduate degree that had been interrupted by the birth of her third son. She attended night school alongside students who were younger than her children, completing her class reading and homework in between our weekend soccer tournaments and in the wee hours of the morning after a late-night bartending shift.

"Why are you going back to college, Mom—you already have a job, so who cares?" I casually asked her one day when I was a carefree high-schooler. She whipped around, put her hands on my shoulders, and looked me squarely in the eyes. "Nothing is more important than an education, nothing. It will open all the doors that your dad and I don't have keys for; it makes impossible things possible, Alexis," she said.

Despite their split, my parents were exceptional co-parents and I sometimes daydreamed about us all living under one roof again. I'd savor little moments after soccer practice, when my dad would be walking on my right side, carrying my soccer bag, and my mom on my left carrying my water bottle. The three of us would walk to one of their cars and I always wondered what it would feel like for all of us to casually slide into the same car and drive home, *together*. I was curious if all kids with divorced parents felt that way or if it was just me.

I used to joke with my friends that my parents' "nonmarriage" was better than the majority of the situations of their parents, who may have been married but not so secretly despised each other. My dad would eventually remarry when I was twelve. Jane—whom I adored—had a daughter already and so I happily inherited my baby sister, Jesse, whom I'd been praying for my whole life. Though I assume some women grow out of it, I seemed to always remain Daddy's little girl.

In elementary school, parents were allowed to eat lunch with their child once a week. Like clockwork, every week, my dad would show up and sit in the little chairs made for five-year-olds, knees pressed uncomfortably up to his chest. On our weekends with him, I remember curling up on his chest, falling asleep to the consistent thudding of his heartbeat as he lay on the couch watching sports with my brothers. His apartment was a small two-bedroom. My brothers Nate and Josh shared a room, sleeping in twin-size trundle beds. I, however, had the luxury of sleeping in a blue and green hammock that hung only a few feet from my dad's bed. At night, he'd stretch out the hammock so he could lay a sheet down, then pick up my little body, lay me in with a pillow, and tuck me in with a cozy blanket. And every night he and I would both be lulled to sleep listening to sports radio.

My dad is as affectionate, gregarious, and outgoing as they come, easily hiding his years of on-again/off-again bouts of depression behind a big smile and warm handshake. As I was growing up, he was an impressive athlete, playing and coaching most of our sports teams. He was also a strict disciplinarian, though he rarely if ever cursed. His anger was quiet and stoic. His vulnerability was nonexistent until much later in life. That said, I was much more scared of disappointing my dad than I was of getting in trouble. That fear kept me on the straight and narrow, most of the time. A rare exception was my dad's actual nightmare coming true—that his fourteen-year-old freshman daughter would attempt sneaking out to attend a senior party with lots of drunk boys. Don't worry. I got busted. Even then, there was no yelling, no ranting. As I walked in, head hanging, he simply said, "I'm so sorry." Clearly I was confused by his apology. He hugged me tight and said it again: "I'm sorry that at any point I've led you to believe that it's okay to lie to get what you want, because it's not. You will be grounded. And I love you so much." He kept hugging me as I bawled my eyes out for having disappointed the man I loved most in the world. What a conundrum to experience unconditional love in a world where human love seemed so very, very conditional.

When we were at my dad's house, we never missed church on Sundays. He helped lead my youth group and he somehow managed to make God cool and relatable to a bunch of greasy-fingered, pizza-eating middle school punks. He personified the bedrock of my faith. My dad undoubtedly saw something he'd learned from his own mother: God for who he or she really was—incomprehensible to our tiny minds; bigger than gender constructs, cultural constructs, and certainly bigger than any book. He understood that building empathy, humility, and gratitude in young people could not be taught in theory. He'd say, "It's hard to imagine walking in someone's shoes if you've never even met the person who puts those shoes on their feet." And so, my siblings and I fed the homeless every Saturday, to make sure we met the owners of those feet.

Dinner at my dad's house was purposeful. We rarely, if ever, talked about the boys I had crushes on or school drama. Instead, we talked about *real* things: complicated and nuanced ideas and current events intentionally presented from various perspectives. I was encouraged to disagree, to ask questions and to offer new thoughts. I was taught that my ideas were valued, expected, and worthy of consideration. I was challenged to think critically, to site my sources, to have well-researched and robust opinions.

In short, my father is to blame for my precociousness. And my mother is to blame for my believing that with a relentless work ethic, impossible things are possible.

————

After my hour of silent reminiscing, my adorable uber driver Jerome put the car in park, which abruptly brought me back to the present. He generously retrieved my suitcase from the trunk and gave me an unexpected bear hug as he said good-bye.

As I stood there long after he'd driven off, unable to process that my childhood as I knew it was in fact untrue . . . the only saving grace was not what but *who* I was coming home to.

CHAPTER THREE

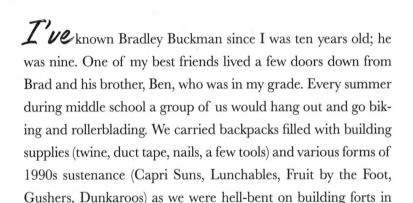

I've known Bradley Buckman since I was ten years old; he was nine. One of my best friends lived a few doors down from Brad and his brother, Ben, who was in my grade. Every summer during middle school a group of us would hang out and go biking and rollerblading. We carried backpacks filled with building supplies (twine, duct tape, nails, a few tools) and various forms of 1990s sustenance (Capri Suns, Lunchables, Fruit by the Foot, Gushers, Dunkaroos) as we were hell-bent on building forts in the surrounding greenbelt.

A saw was eventually "borrowed" from someone's dad and I swear you'd have thought we had struck gold. Up until this point, our sad forts consisted of wooden debris and fallen branches poorly balanced in some sort of tripod that required us crawling in and out on all fours. The idea of a sturdy wooden shelter built from chopped-down trees, not just dead branches, seemed plausible for about thirteen seconds. Because that is all it took for us to realize that sawing down a perfectly healthy mature tree with ten-year-old hands was slightly above our strength grade. That poor tree probably still shakes her leaves at the quarter inch of a slice we made before collectively conceding, then diving into our backpacks, devouring our sugary snacks with a dirty-fingernailed frenzy.

We stayed outside all day, every day, until we were called home for dinner. We also logged endless hours cannonballing into the Buckmans' pool. Painfully self-conscious of my newly forming mosquito-bite breast buds, I dreaded getting out of the cold water. Brad, who because he was Ben's little brother was not cool, would occasionally hover from a safe distance. However, during our swimming escapades, Brad made the perfect towel boy because somehow he was always right there holding one for me the minute I needed it. "Um . . . Alexis, here you go," he'd shyly say. I'd smile back and say, "Thank you," instantly making him blush. Like clockwork, Ben would yell, "Get out of here, Braaaddd," and just like that, my towel savior was gone again.

Despite the hundred-degree Texas summer heat and the Buckmans' non-air-conditioned attic, we once decided that playing spin the bottle up there made complete sense. Of course, Brad—now ten to my eleven—wasn't invited. Ben's first spin landed on me. I hoped that the others would think the perspiration on my top lip was due to the baking heat in the attic and not the anxiety of this being my first kiss. I steeled myself and went in for an appropriate eleven-year-old peck. Ben on the other hand opened his mouth and stuck out his tongue like a screaming goat. The shock of it forced me to break the cardinal rule of kissing. My eyes shot open.

Suddenly, I was making direct eye contact with Ben. Questions flooded my brain: Why were *his* eyes open? And more importantly, why was he trying to swallow me whole? Answers were elusive, so I screamed directly into the mouth of the human hoover attached to my face and then proceeded to run down the stairs in a panic. When I threw open the attic door, I ran smack dab into Brad. Clearly, he'd had his ten-year-old ear pressed against the door in the hopes of vicariously experiencing the exciting and quite terrifying game. We both screamed and then I kept running, flanked by my two closest homegirls.

A few years later, I would have a "real" first kiss with a boy named Charlie. Charlie was a Friday Night Lights, high school cliché: a gorgeous popular football jock who would eventually get paid to model, appearing, ironically, shirtless on shopping bags selling clothes. I fell hard and long. I was so in love that I was able to rationalize what I can now see as textbook red flags. Case in point, despite having a girlfriend asleep upstairs with pinkeye, Charlie justified our first of many hot-tub kisses by explaining that they were maybe, somehow "on a break." That would become something of a pattern—our justified kissing despite his various girlfriends. I understand now with my adult brain how ridiculous my murky fourteen-year-old girl logic was, but God, was I willing to believe anything he said, as long as it ended with more kissing.

Like a ghost, Charlie exists now as only a few remembered snapshots of my faded first love:

Fifteen-year-old Lex walking in Charlie's first-floor hallway. Charlie grabbed me and pressed me against the wall and kissed me until I was breathless. Then he casually walked into the next room to rejoin our friends as though nothing had happened. Given our relationship was kept secret for years, I remember the moment as thrilling and terribly confusing. I prayed we were equally smitten.

Sixteen-year-old Lex studying at Charlie's house. Rather than doing his work, Charlie would just stare at me with those eyes.

I looked at him over my textbook and said, "What?" smirkingly and eager.

"I didn't say anything," he deadpanned.

"Then what are you looking at?" I said, trying not to let my racing heart betray my nerves.

"I'm just looking at you. . . . Is that okay?" He held my gaze until I shyly looked away, officially under the spell of new love.

Seventeen-year-old Lex, standing on the staircase in Charlie's house. I raised my arms high above my head, stretching. A few stairs below me, Charlie was eye level with my stomach. He grabbed my body and kissed my exposed bellybutton. It caught me so off guard that I shrieked as he laughed at my delight. I felt electricity run through my body. This was a dizzying introduction; my as-yet-unexplored sexuality had been awakened.

Charlie went on to be my first everything. And for nearly a decade of my life, I was convinced I would marry him. Given that our older brothers were best friends, I was off-limits to Charlie (and to every other boy who breathed air for that matter). So, initially we hid our love, claiming to everyone else to be nothing more than best friends, *for years*. I can see now that I needed him to set free the wild part of me that I didn't necessarily understand or trust. I fell in love with a boy and he fell right back. We eventually came clean to everyone about our being in a relationship. Nobody was surprised. Our brothers included.

Charlie's family became my own. His mother, Deborah, became a second mom to me, offering guidance during some of the most formative and tumultuous teenage years of my life. His brother, Damon, became my fifth older brother, and his best friends became some of my closest friends. One night at a high school party, one of his best buds, Aiden, had had a bit too much to drink. With his arm thrown affectionately around me and his hot, beery breath in my face, he said, "You know I love Char-Char, and you know I love you, too, right?"

"Yes," I assured him.

"It's just that . . . you will never end up with Charlie," he said.

My smile quickly faded. Even as he could see I was crushed, he doubled down. "You know that, right?" He didn't wait for my reply. He just slid his arm down off my shoulder and began to walk back into the party. Just before he disappeared into the crowd, he said over his shoulder: "Because you'll always deserve better, Jones, and Charlie knows it, too."

I never forgot his best friend stating such a cold truth on that warm Texas night. I've wondered over the years if he ever remembered saying it, if he actually believed it or if he just thought he was giving me some kind of backhanded compliment. Either way, it always felt like a pebble in my shoe: a nagging, uncomfortable bit of foreshadowing. I think my heart knew it to be true, but my mind stubbornly refused to accept it because love has a profound way of trumping logic.

Aiden wasn't the only one who tried to warn me against Charlie. Despite my being a grade younger, Charlie and I were in a pre-calculus class together. Our teacher, Mrs. Harper, once witnessed him copying my homework, as I undoubtedly stared at him adoringly. She held me after class, clearly feeling compelled to say something. He had, after all, turned in a blank pop quiz with a message in all caps that said, "Dear Pretty, Pretty Princess . . ." and then he proceeded to say something along the lines of, "I had a big game last night and am not prepared to take this quiz but look forward to retaking it tomorrow. Thanks for understanding my demanding football schedule." Needless to say, Mrs. H was not under the same love spell as me. There was no rescheduled quiz. With a much-deserved eye roll, she promptly gave him a zero.

Mrs. H was my favorite teacher and mentor. She was young, beautiful, and cool. Which in truth made her advice sting even more. "Alexis, I hate to say this because I know you really like him, but here's the deal; it's fine to date a 'Charlie' [she used air quotes for his name] but you never want to *marry* a Charlie," she said flatly.

My expression must have been one of hurt and confusion. She went on: "It's just that . . . you don't want to marry the guy who peaks in high school." Then she softly patted me on the back and reminded me of the test we were having at the end of the week. My teenager brain decided she was right about a lot of things, but clearly dead wrong on this one.

Charlie and I eventually went to the same college and our romance ramped up. We talked about all our dreams together, post-graduation. Once, as we soaked together in a bathtub, he said, "Alexis, you know I'm going to marry you, right?" I just smiled because it didn't warrant a response. Of course he was. I'd been practicing writing his last name in cursive in the back of my Trapper Keeper notebook since I was in middle school. My entire idea of love began and ended with his obnoxiously beautiful face.

But the dysfunction ramped up in college, too. We broke up and got back together countless times. The being on "breaks" justifications he'd used with me were unsurprisingly now used *on* me. He consistently cheated on me. I consistently found out—sadly, always from his closest friends or roommates. I once made up a fake email account to catch him in lies and properly accost him—anonymously—because I was a coward. He found out it was me. I was mortified. I looked like an insecure, obsessive, lovesick girlfriend. Because that is *exactly* what I was, a twenty-year-old girl white knuckling a doomed, star-crossed love all the while, praying for a different outcome to an already written tragedy.

We clearly had trust issues, but I, like others before me, chose to ignore them. So, while Charlie may have been "hooking up" other girls here and there, he always assured me that I was different, I was "the one." (Sitting next to me as I type, Gussie—my French bulldog—just exhaled loudly and with exasperation. My sentiments exactly, Gussie. Lordy, the things we are willing to believe when we are young and so very much in love.)

Eventually our foundation was not simply cracked; there were jackhammer-sized holes that were becoming irreparable. I was angry at how brave I could be in life and how insecure I could be in love, bypassing righteous indignation and sacred anger, swallowing my own voice and smothering my intuition time after time. Charlie felt like the one exception to every rule I had for myself. The drug I couldn't seem to quit.

So we unintentionally broke each other's hearts. And then like a cosmic compulsion, we'd always find our way back to each other, each time our love a little more damaged than before.

Years later, a hard-sought-out truth from my surrogate big brother and his actual brother, Damon, would put the final nail in the coffin of the Charlie saga, which was still unfolding even after I finished graduate school.

Charlie was then living in San Diego. Even with the continued on-again, off-again nature of whatever we were, I was still convinced that Charlie was "the one," so I drove down from Los Angeles to visit him any chance I could. But after I'd returned from a two-week work trip abroad, he ghosted me. Charlie's last words to me before I'd left were "I love you. Hurry back." But all my calls now went unreturned. At first, I was genuinely concerned when I didn't hear from him. Days, then weeks, and then months passed. No call, no text. Nothing. I was confused. Then I became angry and deeply ashamed that after all these years I was still allowing myself to be hurt yet again, by the same guy.

I returned home to Austin at one point and went to a concert with old friends. It was there that I heard a painful rumor: Charlie had gotten a girl pregnant. It sounded outlandish. I knew that if I called Damon, he would confirm that it was in fact silly hometown gossip. I called him repeatedly from my car, finally waking him up. I told him what I'd just heard. His response was a devastating silence, which spoke volumes.

"Fuck," Damon finally said. "He told me he was going to tell you. God, I'm so sorry this is how you're finding out."

"Wait. What? I don't understand . . . why wouldn't he have told me?" I choked out.

"Honestly Lex, what could he possibly say?"

For several minutes, I didn't move. I had never sat so still in my life. It felt like my heart had shattered so completely that only fine dust remained in its place.

The concert had ended well after midnight, but I didn't want to go home. All I could think to do was drive to a church parking lot to be alone with my thoughts, and possibly with God. I figured if God existed, I needed Her to help explain what in the hell was going on and how I could possibly live in a world in which Charlie was not my person, something that in that moment felt utterly inconceivable.

God didn't have a ready explanation—at least that I could hear. I spent the next hour taking turns screaming into my steering wheel and hyperventilating-crying. I wasn't just grieving the death of the most monumental relationship in my life. I was grieving the fucking *certainty* I thought I had about him being my person, the future we'd talked about, the kids we'd imagined, the decade I now felt I'd wasted loving him, and the idea that I might now have to give up Deb and Damon, too. I didn't know who I was or who I could be without Charlie. My heart ached so badly—physically—that I thought it might stop altogether. Part of me welcomed the possibility.

Over the next few hours, weeks, and years, I vacuumed up every single dust particle of my combusted heart. Looking back, I unconsciously and unfairly sought Charlie's love and validation as the source of my confidence because I hadn't yet learned how to do that for myself. I eventually dated again—unintentionally breaking some hearts of my own—but nothing stuck. I spent years wondering if I'd ever love or be loved with the kind of fucked-up ferocity and passion that defined my relationship with Charlie. I watched my friends find the love of their lives, get married, start families, and I feared maybe there was no one out there for me after all.

Now to be clear, the reason Charlie gets mentioned in this story at all is because without my first love, I would have never found my way to my *great* love. Plus, I'm a firm believer that our "love stories" should encompass all of our loves, not just the one we end up with. In other words, it's important to remember that the road to Great Love is oftentimes complicated, messy, painful, and surprisingly serendipitous. Indeed, it was *another* call from Charlie's brother, Damon, that would change the entire trajectory of my life. Again.

"Hey, Little Jones," he said over the phone one night when I was home in Austin. "I really want you to come out, meet my new girlfriend . . . and [wait for it] . . . also, I think I just met your person."

I ended up grieving the loss of Deb—Charlie's mom, my second mom—longer and harder than I ever did him. Fortunately, Damon remained a surrogate big brother. Over the years, I'd asked Damon if he knew any great guys he could set me up with—which always ended in some version of him shrugging and saying nope. Which means that Damon calling to say he knew someone he might actually recommend was a huge change of heart. I should have been thrilled. But I was exhausted and in no mood to meet anyone, much less my person.

I happened to be home from Los Angeles because my dad was in a life-threatening battle with not one, but two kinds of cancer: lymphoma and multiple myeloma. He had already done a year of chemotherapy for the lymphoma and was now getting a bone marrow transplant from an anonymous donor to treat the myeloma. Rather than be in LA captaining the ship of an organization I'd started in college, I was driving back and forth between Austin and the MD Anderson medical center in Houston, where my dad was being treated. I didn't know how long I'd have to be working this way, but my dad's odds of survival were not good, so I wanted to soak up as much time with him and the rest of my family as I could.

Despite the terrible timing, Damon gently persuaded me to meet him on the condition that he would drop the setup idea and I could just come out to meet his new lady friend. But minutes after I arrived at the bar, Damon went back on his word. He grabbed me and pointed to the back of a very, very tall guy.

"That's the guy I was talking about," he whispered loudly.

Seconds later, this giant let out a belly laugh, and there I was, standing face-to-face with Ben Buckman's *little* brother, Brad. All I could think was, *Dear Baby Jesus, when did that scrawny towel boy grow up and get hot?*

Years earlier in college, I was playing darts and drinking beer at a dive bar near USC. It was the NCAA college basketball Final Four. My hometown team—the University of Texas—was playing Syracuse on TV. Out of the corner of my eye I saw a handsome face on the screen just as the announcer summed up some stats: "Buckman with fourteen points, seven rebounds," he said dramatically. I sat straight up on my bar stool and said to no one and everyone, "Wow, good for him!"

The bartender had been watching, too, and asked me if I knew Brad Buckman, the kid on TV.

"Yeah," I said a little nostalgically and with my eyes still locked on Brad. "I grew up with him and honestly he might be the kindest person I have ever met." I hadn't seen Brad much since I graduated high school but in all the interactions we had had since childhood, that was the only and very specific feeling I had about him: that he was uncommonly kind.

Now, Brad slowly made his way through the crowded bar to come talk to Damon (who was dating his best friend's little sister) and me. It suddenly seemed that our roles had reversed. I was now the awkward one, fumbling for words. "Um . . . Hi . . . Brad . . . wow . . . you're so . . . grown up." This late bloomer, who was shy and didn't say much more to me in high school than an awkward hi, was home briefly from his exotic life of playing professional basketball in Europe and had become the picture of calm, cool, and collected. Whereas I remembered a high-pitched, cracking voice from our adolescence, now Brad's voice was low and steady and sexy, even as it evoked the same humility and kindness I remembered.

"Hi Alexis. Wow, you look beautiful. How are you?"

My next thought was that this man, not boy, was using complete sentences. I hoped I could do the same. Damon looked at me, pointing at Brad from behind mouthing, "Right?!" clearly proud of his Cupidity.

Over the next few hours, Brad and I talked sports and flirted. I playfully threw ice from my drink at my new buddy as I argued that USC should have won the 2005 Rose Bowl and how I knew Vince Young was never going to make it in the big leagues. Then we switched to more meaningful banter. I had just unapologetically finished a passionate rant about the collective resentment generations of women have felt over compromising their careers and their well-being to meet the standards of a motherhood steeped in martyrdom when Brad rather bluntly said, "You like to talk."

"Geez, I like to talk?! Yes, Brad, I'm a human being that talks," I said, sounding slightly offended.

Brad had unintentionally struck a nerve. As a young girl there was a sharp edge to the warm halo affixed to me. I remember a classmate's dad barking at my mom in the grocery store parking lot. "She's cute, Claudia, but she's too damn aggressive. You need to do something about that." I'd told my mom how a boy tattled on me, complaining I was "playing too hard" when I pegged him in the head for the win in a school-wide dodgeball game.

"She's not aggressive, Tommy, she's passionate about everything she does. And she's got a hell of a right arm, huh? Speaking of, how's your little guy doing?" she said sympathetically. He grumbled something and said, "He's fine, thanks," as he stormed off.

My mom turned to me and stated with confidence, "Boys have never known what to do with a strong girl and men don't have any better ideas when you become a woman. They are going to complain and call you 'too much this or not enough that,' so let them. Because you're never going to fit neatly into whatever box they want to shove you in." I'd spent most my life trying to prove my mom wrong. It would take me years to realize that she wasn't. Turns out a strong woman is a mysterious riddle to most men, and it isn't our job to offer people clues in the footnotes.

At this point in my life, I'd grown accustomed to all the men who had wanted to date "empowered women," *in theory*. In the few dating escapades I had experienced post Charlie, I'd had one Ivy League soccer player shame me for not being a virgin, a trust fund kid tell me he wasn't okay with me ever "making more money than him," and a winemaker who shamed me for wanting to have *too much* sex. Dating was confusing. And given the dire situation with my father, at the moment I didn't have the energy to accommodate any guy's opinion of me. I was simply too tired. So, Brad—for better or worse—was getting a rather rare, unvarnished version of me.

"Oh no, I didn't mean it like that," Brad said in response to my prickling. He proceeded to clarify. "This is going to sound weird, but I think my mom is the strongest woman I have ever met. And I've never met anyone as opinionated as her . . . well . . . until *you*," he said, almost with a sense of awe.

Here I was, maybe for the first time in my life, being radically "me" and this guy was not only interested but impressed?

Leaning close, he went on: "I could listen to you talk for hours."

"Really?" I said, timidly. "To be honest, I think I talk too much."

"I don't!" he said, abruptly sitting up straight and now looking offended himself.

"Why would you say that? You don't talk too much. You should never apologize for having a lot to say and caring as deeply as you do. It's actually really hot," he said. His voice now mirrored my vulnerability.

He quickly looked self-conscious. He followed up as if his last statement needed clarification. "Sorry, by 'hot' I mean, it's just really cool. I mean . . . I respect it . . . I respect you. . . . Shit. I'm not as good with words as you are." He looked down at his drink. There was the adorable, shy boy I remembered from high school. I reached for his hand and gently squeezed it.

"Thank you. That actually means a lot," I said as we cautiously made eye contact. For the next several hours, I watched him watch me as I told more stories and went on more rants. Every time, I glanced at him, he was smiling at me, like he knew something I didn't, but wasn't ready to tell me.

Brad and I exchanged numbers that night and a few days later went on a first date to a local sushi restaurant. When we had sat down, ordered, and had almost polished off our first drink, Brad put all his cards on the table.

"I'm not even gonna try and play it cool," he said, grinning ear to ear. Then, as though he'd taken a bite of something that was piping hot and that he just had to spit out, he confessed, "Alexis, I've been in love with you since I was nine years old."

Seeing the shock on my face, he quickly elaborated. "Wow. Okay, so here's the deal, obviously no pressure. Even if I never get a second date or ever hear from you after tonight, I just wanted you to know I am freaking out inside because I'm living out my dream of being on a date with my childhood crush, that's all."

I was a little stunned not by how much he'd just shared but with the confidence and vulnerability he'd displayed in doing so. For once, words failed me. To hide my discomfort, I laughed awkwardly and told him I hoped I wouldn't disappoint him. He assured me that I simply couldn't—he was happy enough to even be on this one date.

Whatever this was, I was a little scared by how different— and yet comfortable—it felt. The waiter arrived at just that moment and admitted that he knew who Brad was; he'd been a UT basketball fan his whole life. Brad ordered dinner and another round of drinks, and the moment relaxed. We proceeded to eat and talk for hours. We told stories from our shared childhood and laughed so hard, the dimples in my cheeks started to cramp.

We finally realized that we were the last diners in the place and the staff was ready to go home. Brad looked at me and smiled. I felt drunk off that smile. Although, to be fair, I was also tipsy. Moments later, his smile softened a bit and he just looked at me intently. I felt like he had X-ray vision and he could see all the damaged parts of me, the scars from previous relationships, and he wanted to speak directly to them.

"Alexis," he said, "if I were dating anyone or interested in anyone before tonight . . . I am no longer. I don't want you to wonder whether there is anyone else because you . . . *you* have my full attention for however long we are exploring whatever this could be."

This was so novel for me. He wasn't awkward or shifty, he didn't look away, he didn't crack a joke. There was no agenda here except honesty. His intentions were crystal fucking clear. Once again, I was left overwhelmed by the integrity, courage, and vulnerability of the man now standing before me, holding my jacket.

We walked to another bar just so the night didn't have to end. An hour into yet more stories and more belly laughs, we experienced a lull in the conversation, and I thought he might be thinking about leaning over to kiss me. We both looked down and laughed awkwardly and then the moment passed. Or so I thought. When Brad looked up again, he smiled and said "Fuck it" as he placed his hands on either side of my face and leaned in to kiss me. I don't know what I was expecting—though I did hope he didn't have the same technique as his brother had in middle school—but Mr. Brad Buckman surpassed my expectations. His lips were soft, the perfect amount of pressure and tenderness.

"You thought I missed my window, didn't you?" Brad said with a sarcastic confidence. "But I didn't," he said, obviously proud of himself.

"To be clear, you kinda did," I jabbed playfully back.

Then, with a competitive confirmation that he'd nailed our first kiss, I added, "Don't get me wrong, Buckman, you totally made up for it."

"What can I say, you gotta shoot your shots, babe," he said as he laughed and made a basketball shooting motion with his hands.

"Babe?" I replied, with flirty sass. "I mean, are we there yet?"

Without hesitation he said, "Umm, yeah, I think we're there," bringing out the perfect balance of hot athlete swagger to accompany his kindness and vulnerability. I snuggled up closer to him with my flirty eyes and alcohol-warmed cheeks to let him know that I was clearly into whatever shots he was shooting.

At closing time, neither of us wanted the night to end so we agreed to go to his house. Once there we talked and kissed for hours and all I could think was that this had to be a world-record for the longest and best first date. In the early hours of the morning, Brad got up from the couch to go to the bathroom and I made a bold move. I quickly stripped down to my underwear and tried to figure out a way to sit sexily on his bed. When Brad came back from the bathroom and saw me, his eyes widened like a deer in the headlights. I watched as his eyes lowered to stare straight at my boobs, then back to my eyes, then back to my boobs, then he abruptly turned around so that his back was to me and he was facing the wall. I was confused. *This isn't how it goes in the movies*, I thought.

My confusion morphed into horror as I realized I must have grossly misread the situation. This was all new to me. I had always been such a prude. I rarely kissed on a first date. I had certainly never hooked up on a first date, much less faced cold, hard rejection. I crossed my arms over my chest and started to think about what to put back on first and how quickly I could make an escape.

Brad broke the silence. "Umm . . . Lex, don't get me wrong . . . I have literally waited seventeen years to see your boobs and . . . well . . . Gawd they are awesome," he said, half turning around again to look, but then he stopped himself.

"It's just that I think we have had a lot to drink tonight . . . and I really, really like you. Also, I figure if you know I can walk away from the greatest temptation of my life, like literally my dream girl half dressed in my bed, you won't ever wonder about whether I can walk away from temptation in the future." He paused for my reaction but I was experiencing an internal shame spiral and couldn't think straight.

"So, if you're okay with it," he said gently, "I think we should call it for tonight," which in truth felt less like a question and more like a statement.

I was speechless. Like most women, I had spent years trying to get guys *not* to sexualize me, *not* to objectify me, *not* to assume my kindness was an invitation or permission for their sexual advances. And here was Brad doing what? Respecting me and making sure I had all my faculties about me before we escalated things, even after I'd made the move to escalate them? I was beyond embarrassed. Tears of shame brimmed in my eyes, and I hugged my arms tightly around my nudity.

Brad wasn't deterred. He went to his closet, grabbed one of his giant T-shirts, and quickly put it over my head. Then he hugged my tense body with one arm and—given his massive wingspan—turned out the light with the other. We sat like that for a while and eventually laid down. I cried quiet tears of gratitude. I had never known that kind of self-restraint, that kind of protection, that kind of love, that kind of respect, or this kind of man.

I slept in Brad's arms all night and woke up with a killer hangover and seething shame from humiliating drunken rejection. I thought maybe I could just keep my eyes closed and avoid seeing him altogether, but a girl can't sleep forever in a bed that is not hers. So, I finally opened one mascara-smeared eyelid to assess the situation. My dehydrated tongue felt the velvety fur on my teeth, reminding me that I had not brushed them the night before. I was certain that my morning breath would have made a week-old corpse smell sweet.

Damnit if Brad wasn't staring at me with an adorable toothy grin. Not thirty seconds into my being awake and he dove in headfirst with "I don't want you to feel bad about last night. It's not that I don't want to sleep with you, it's just that I want to be honest: I have motives." He paused for dramatic effect.

"It's that I want to sleep with you over and over and over

again, for a very long time." God, that smile. I couldn't help but blush despite my splitting headache.

"But until we get to that chapter of us . . . I'm not going to play games and not call you for three days to make you wonder if I like you. I'd like to take you to breakfast if you'll let me."

I didn't move. I politely smiled, holding my breath in hopes that he wouldn't smell it. "Okay, I'll take that as a yes! I'll be downstairs if you want to shower and change, well . . . back into your clothes . . . from your attempt to sleep with me on the first date!" he said in a mockingly scandalous tone.

I pulled the covers over my head.

"Sorry . . . too soon? Hey, I have a whole pack of new toothbrushes, I'll leave one for you on the counter. Take your time. Seriously, no rush." He kissed my cheek and a few minutes later he was about to shut the bedroom door when he poked his head back in and said, "Alexis Jones is in my bed. Holy shit."

Every time I think of that night, I'm reminded of a scene in the 2012 movie *The Perks of Being a Wallflower*. A young high school kid asks his favorite teacher why nice people seem to choose the wrong people to date. "Because," says the teacher, "we accept the love we think we deserve." In that moment, I remember trying to understand why I had felt I deserved so little for so long.

I'll skip the continued play-by-play and press fast forward: Breakfast turned into all day and all day turned into me moving to Spain, then Germany, then Turkey with him while he continued playing professional European basketball and I wrote my first book, *I Am That Girl*. Then "we" turned into the rest of my life.

It wasn't always smooth sailing, though. Two years into dating, I kept thinking the other shoe was about to drop. Brad was trying to settle my nerves after bringing up the idea of marriage. Sitting in a parking lot, I kept telling him all the reasons both logical and utterly ridiculous of why marriage was a bad idea and that I'd much prefer just *dating* him for the rest of my life.

"Alexis, I know you're scared of marriage. You spent almost a decade loving someone who broke your heart. Then half a decade dating boys who made you feel small to make themselves feel big. Your mom was married five times. Shit, your grandmother was married nine times. It makes sense, baby, that a lifelong commitment doesn't seem possible. So, I'm not asking you *not* to be scared, that would be unrealistic. I know there are no guarantees in life. We could try and we could fail. I guess I'm just asking you to be scared with *me*," he explained.

He was right. I *was* terrified of love. I was terrified of it going so terribly wrong again, burning me up entirely. I was petrified of him ripping out my heart and my being left in an existential state of dissolution all over again, especially when I'd worked so hard to put myself back together after the initial combustion. But if he was still choosing to love me when I was cynical at best, then I figured I could give my best friend and the best sex of my life a chance at forever.

If any doubts remained about him being my person, he silenced them with a subsequent conversation. Newly engaged, we were sitting at a restaurant and out of the blue he said, "I want you to know it doesn't bother me that you still love Charlie." I stared at him in mild shock. I wasn't quite sure where this was going. "It's just that he was your best friend and your first love, and I know how much he meant to you." He took a sip of wine.

"You see, I don't believe love is finite, that your love for him or anyone else you've dated takes anything away from the love you have for me. I think love is an infinite ocean and the love you hold for him and others . . . well, it says everything about you and nothing about them. I love the depth by which you love, and one day," he said with the wineglass still in his hand, "I will shake Charlie's hand and thank him . . . not for breaking your heart, of course. I would thank him and all your other past loves for helping shape the girl into the woman I now get to spend the rest of my life with . . . the great love of my life."

If I was stunned before, I was utterly speechless now.

"Shit," Brad continued. "The greatest gift those guys ever gave me was walking away from you, because Lord knows I never could," he said, shaking his head.

If I was stunned and then speechless before, now I was just simply in awe. In awe of Brad's generosity of spirit. In awe of his self-confidence. In awe of his expansive love. It's not as though I had been erasing Charlie from stories of my earlier years—he and his family had been so much a part of the fabric of my life that I had certainly mentioned them from time to time—but now I saw that Brad didn't need me to diminish the role Charlie or any other past relationship had played in my life to make himself feel more comfortable or confident. Brad refused to ignore the first act of my play, pretending that my life started when he entered the scene; instead, he magnanimously welcomed the

entire cast, even if past costars left the stage long before he arrived.

For years I had wondered what the point of the painful
decade-long Charlie saga was, feeling as though there was some
essential closure I had been denied. I desperately wanted and
longed for an explanation from someone clearly incapable or
unwilling to give it to me, thinking it would release me from my
painful heartbreak. I'd ping-pong back and forth, wondering if
him walking away from me so easily meant he was a coward,
that he just didn't care, or that maybe all that time, he never
really loved me as much as I loved him. Eventually, I realized it
actually didn't matter. Charlie would never be able to give me
the closure, compassion, and grace only I could offer my younger
self. In letting go of him, I was finally learning how to love myself. For if it's true, that our capacity to love others directly cor-
relates with our ability to love ourselves, then I had to look at
why I'd been depriving myself of the fortune I clearly possessed.

Eventually the purpose of my pain was revealed: with no
heartbreak Charlie, there would be no brother Damon, and
with no Damon there would be no reintroduction to Brad. And
with no Brad, there would be no Great Love recorded in the history book of my life. For so many years, I thought I belonged
with Charlie, but then I realized you can't belong to anyone until
you belong to yourself first. And I hadn't figured out how to do
that yet. Charlie was an important pitstop in the bumpy, broken
road of my love journey, and there were certainly a few more
stops after him, but they were all leading me straight to Brad—
because unbeknownst to me, he was always going to be my final

destination. Everyone else was just the warmup acts; Brad was the headliner.

Our most painful teachers are often our most important lessons. I will forever be grateful to Charlie because he taught me one of the most significant lessons of my life: that there is *always* purpose to our pain and time is the only revealer.

CHAPTER FOUR

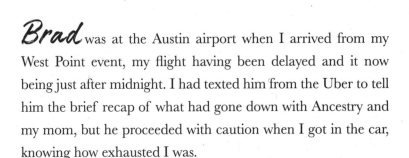

Brad was at the Austin airport when I arrived from my West Point event, my flight having been delayed and it now being just after midnight. I had texted him from the Uber to tell him the brief recap of what had gone down with Ancestry and my mom, but he proceeded with caution when I got in the car, knowing how exhausted I was.

"You want to talk about it, babe?" he said tenderly.

"Umm . . . not really," I said as I shrugged my shoulders in the passenger seat, looking out the window. Trying to justify my emotional withdrawal, I simply offered, "It's a lot, ya know?"

They say when it rains it pours, but the news about my dad felt more like a tsunami had been casually added to the weather report after I'd already been pummeled by what felt like a particularly horrendous hurricane season.

In recent years I felt like my very public career had been on an explosive, exponential upward trajectory. I'd seen early success while at graduate school at USC founding my first female empowerment company, I AM THAT GIRL. Then there were the awards and accolades I'd earned, including winning a Jefferson Award (the highest national honor for public service), being featured as one of Oprah's SuperSoul100, being an Ambassador for L'Oreal's STEM initiative, being featured as one of Fast Company's "Female Trailblazers," being named one of ESPN's "Pop Culture's Top Ten," and receiving the Girl Scouts' Women of Distinction award. While it all made me sound amazing in theory, I still slept in oversized granny panties, slurred with my nighttime retainer in, and ate cereal for dinner because I'm someone who burns boiling water. I quickly learned that no number of awards can make the uncool parts of you cool. If anything, I had developed an appetite for shiny gold stars and no amount of them could satiate me. External success had also conveniently been a highly effective camouflage for all the insecurities hidden underneath.

The truth was, I was hanging on by a thread at this point in my life and no one knew it more intimately than Brad. I had stopped being honest with friends and most of my family when they asked how I was doing, because I was ashamed that I was struggling so much when I felt like I was supposed to be the poster girl for empowerment. And deep down, I felt if I wasn't entertaining people with sparkly achievements and audacious endeavors, then they'd simply have no use for me. What an elaborate little tale I had spun to maintain the narrative of the "not-enough-ness" I felt deep within. To be fair, it's much easier to see it now, looking back, than while I was in it.

When I was five years old, my mother enrolled me in dance

class. The teacher announced we were going to have a "smile competition," to see who could smile the longest during a run-through of our upcoming performance. That word "competition" awoke something inside me. I felt my eyes narrow, a smirk spread across my face, and my body relaxed as though I'd waited my entire life for someone to present me with a starting line. She said "Go" and I smiled with such conviction that my dimples eventually began to burn and even started twitching from muscle fatigue. After what felt like a lifetime but was probably less than ten minutes, I began welling up with tears from the physical discomfort but gawddamnit I wouldn't quit. I don't think I could have if I tried. I had my brothers in the back of my head. I wanted to win. I wanted them to be proud of me.

Finally, as if I had been held underwater, convulsing from lack of oxygen, she relieved my anguish-filled smile.

"Okay, you can stop smiling now. And the winner is . . . Alexis."

I suppose this was the first moment that I put two and two together; pain was part of the package when it came to victory and success; striving, winning, performing, proving would always bear an expensive tax. A tax that was absolutely worth it.

Sadly, this is the only memory I have of my dance class as a child. No giggling, no silliness, no shamelessly uncoordinated leaps or frenetic happy-feet dances. I won my first gold star that day, and my dance teacher gave me my first hit of external validation. I knew exactly what I wanted, and it was more shiny stars. Little did I know that no amount of those sacred five-pointed twinklers would fill the Milky Way–sized hole inside of me of not feeling like I was enough. Striving for validation would be the dangling carrot, driving me for the next several decades of my life.

———

When I was growing up, Grandma Bess insisted that my mom buy a house in a neighborhood that my parents could "afford." But my mom refused to accept the academically inferior schools in the school district that was in my parents' very modest budget. She told me once about an exchange she had with my grandmother.

"Claudia," Bess said, "you have to think about those kids. It will be so much harder on them, being the poorest kids in the school district. They will never feel like they fit in."

My mom rarely dug her heels in, especially when it came to Bess, but apparently this time was one of them.

"Damn it, Bess. The *only* thing I ever think about is my kids. And yes, it will be hard on them. Your son and I will have to work that much harder so that they don't *feel* less, just because they *have* less. I wish to God we could give them more, I really do. But what we can give them is access to the best education possible and trust that they will create opportunities for themselves that their dad and I simply can't offer them," my mom said emphatically. My grandmother quickly realized this was not a discussion and, as my mom tells it, she dropped it.

Buying a home in Westlake, one of the wealthiest and best

school districts in Austin, was certainly not an option for our family financially. So, in the spare time my mother never had, she would drive up and down the streets looking for For Rent signs in Cuernavaca, the one neighborhood in Westlake's school district that we could afford. At the time, it consisted of "unsightly" mobile homes instead of tennis courts, and rabid dogs and broken-down cars instead of manicured lawns, sidewalks, and HOA guidelines.

Eventually my mom found an inexpensive rental house that unlocked the potential of the schools she coveted, effectively making us the "kids from the other side of the tracks." We now lived alongside the rest of the "help," who routinely cleaned the houses and mowed the lawns of the privileged kids I'd eventually befriend. When I got on the school bus, I would often be greeted by a wealthy bully and his followers chanting "Cuerni-rats, Cuerni-rarts . . ." I grimaced in silence while staring out the window, pretending like I couldn't hear them, as my fists balled up in shameful anger, wanting to punch all of them in their stupid, entitled, rich faces.

The one time I missed the bus to school, my mom ignored my false pleas of illness and protests and insisted on driving me in her 1976 jaundice-colored Chevy Malibu that she bought for $500 cash. While my friends were jamming out to Third Eye Blind in their dads' Mercedeses, I was lying down in the backseat, hiding from embarrassment. As she pulled up closer, my cheeks grew flushed, my scalp prickly with sweat. Attempting to exit the car unnoticed, I didn't even wait for it to stop. I jumped

out, did a quick summersault to offset the momentum difference, and sprinted into school, praying to God my outrageous
exit from a moving car might have gone undetected.

Eventually, of course, I got a first-rate education, both academically and socially. Straddling the world I came from and the
world I frequented among many of my friends called for some
skilled navigation. Like when it came to talking about family
vacations, I'd come up with clever ways to circle around the
truth.

"We're staying at our house in Aspen and going skiing for
spring break. Lex, where is your family going?" someone might
ask me at lunch.

"Oh, crazy, we were going to go there too, but something
came up last minute at my dad's company, so we're staying closer
to home this year," I'd casually offer, hoping it didn't trigger too
many follow-up questions. I mean, my dad did technically work
for a company as a structural engineer at the University of
Texas, and maybe how it was worded, it *might* have sounded like
it was *his* company, so it wasn't technically a lie, I'd justify to
myself.

The truth was that our spring break usually consisted of my
mom finding some kind of public swimming hole that was
within three hours of our home. She'd pack up lunches and we'd
go on an adventure to swim for the day. Sun-kissed and maybe
a little carsick, we'd return home each night to avoid restaurant
prices and hotel costs; sleeping in our own beds didn't cost a
cent more than the rent my mom was already scraping by to try
and cover.

We lived in eight houses before I graduated from high school, all but one apartment in Cuernavaca. I asked my mom years later, "Why *did* we move so much?" She thought about it for a minute. "At the time, there was a boom of house buyers, and it seemed like every rental house we lived in was eventually offered a sale deal they couldn't pass up, so we'd be given thirty days' notice to find a new place. All your brothers' friends would show up to help us move, getting paid in pizza. They really took care of us," she said with some nostalgia. "One time we were so broke we couldn't even afford the boxes to move, so we moved our entire house in big black plastic garbage bags. That move was particularly humbling," she said, shaking her head.

After a few moments, my mom continued: "I hated that for you and your brothers, Alexis. All that moving, the shitty cars I drove, the dumpy houses we lived in, and all the clothes I couldn't afford to buy you. You were such a trouper, but I know how hard it was on you.

"I know you never went hungry—in the literal sense—and I'm proud and grateful for that," she said. "But with all the teasing, you just became hungry in other ways, maybe insatiably when I think about it. As a mom, I saw all that hurt, insecurity, and inferiority transform into jet fuel. I sometimes wonder if we hadn't struggled so much financially living in *that* community, would you have accomplished as much as you have? Who would you have become if you weren't hell-bent on proving something to all those kids who made fun of you growing up?" A sheepish smile spread across my face and I thought to myself, *I guess, we'll never know.*

I thought back to a conversation I had had with my brother Josh. I was devastated I wasn't getting a brand-new car when I turned sixteen like all my friends and was undoubtedly pouting. He was home from college when he pulled me aside. "I know our family doesn't have a lot of money, but we have more love in this family than any one I know. People would give anything to have what we have. We are wealthy in love. And it's the only kind of rich that actually matters," he said as he hugged me in tight. He was right. We might have been broke financially, but we were billionaires . . . in love. Even if my teenage brain agreed entirely and even if it would become some of the most significantly impactful advice in my life, in that moment, it didn't make me want my own set of wheels any less.

Married to Brad for several years now and professionally successful beyond my wildest dreams, my life was unrecognizable from the financial insecurity I'd known as a kid (and spent my adult life fighting to get away from). Things looked simply remarkable from the outside and in so many ways they were. My social media posts highlighted my privileged life—at this point I'd founded not one, but two companies. I also had a lucrative speaking career. And yes, I still wore granny panties. We already went over this. My uncool parts remained intact.

However, social media posts were not conveying the truth of everything unseen: Energy drinks were my chosen method of staying awake, but no amount of caffeine seemed to be doing the job these days. My somewhat manageable anxiety had become utterly debilitating. I was also becoming more and more concerned about the fact that Brad and I had been trying to get pregnant for several years now, but we were still at zilch in the baby department. After months of testing, our infertility challenges were confirmed. The diagnosis, with no explanation as to *why*, was that I apparently had a shockingly low egg count. Something that no amount of grit, determination, desire, or effort could change.

It seemed like there was this perfect life I presented to the world and then this invisible, insecure version of me I shamefully hid. The chasm between the two mes—the one I shared with the public and the one I revealed in private—was growing bigger each day. Behind the velvety red curtain of my illustrious life, I felt like my body, my mind, my soul were quite literally breaking apart; the tectonic plates in my life were no longer willing to cooperate. With the stress of being on the road more than three-quarters of the year, a mysterious neck pain had become so excruciating that I was finding it hard to function at all. Despite numerous X-rays, MRIs, acupuncture, massage therapy, and chiropractor appointments, no doctor could give me more than the vague advice to take better care of myself. I desperately wanted someone to fix the neck problem *for* me because I refused to stop the not-so-ironic-neck-breaking velocity at which I was operating. Ahem.

Knowing I was one sneeze away from a breakdown, I had started seeing a therapist, Dr. Carlos. "Alexis, if you took any one of the things you are dealing with right now individually— your obscene work schedule, your infertility challenges, your debilitating anxiety, your physical pain—it would bring anyone to their knees." He paused, hoping that his concern would sink in.

"But all at once, my dear, it's simply too much." And this was just weeks *before* the biological father bomb was dropped into my lap. I just sat there nodding unemotionally, because it's not like I disagreed. I was just so overwhelmed by it all that I didn't know where to begin. I didn't know how to slow down the bullet train I was on, let alone stop it. I knew I needed to make changes to my life. That was the easy part.

Most people know they need to lose weight, or to drink less, or to break up with the person they know is wrong for them, or to quit the job with the asshole boss, or to move out of the house, or to get the divorce; it's just that actually *doing* those big, hard, and often emotionally and financially complicated things requires energy, clarity, confidence, faith, and willpower.

I knew my life was off-kilter and had been for years now. I knew I was working too much, sleeping too little, that my self-care was nonexistent and my mental health had plummeted. I recognized the hypocrisy in the fact that I preached about the importance of self-care to others and yet didn't integrate the same philosophy into my own life. I knew I needed to slow down, to rest and to rejuvenate. And yet all this "knowing" changed nothing. Because I was too tired to conceive of turning my life upside down.

So, I chose the path of least resistance—as much work as it was to drag my enormous suitcase filled with shit I didn't want to deal with into the next day, doing that seemed easier than actually dealing with it. And every day I'd promise myself that tomorrow . . . tomorrow, I'd handle it. Tomorrow, I'd figure it out. Tomorrow, I'd put together a game plan. Tomorrow is the perfect closet to jam everything into because tomorrow never comes; the closet door can stay safely closed a little while longer.

So, no. I didn't know how I could possibly add uncovering a massive family secret regarding my origin story to the mix. I had so many not-so-tiny fires going on simultaneously that addressing the now raging wildfire of my paternity didn't even feel conceivable.

———

In the less than twenty-four hours that I was home from my West Point event, my mom had called me multiple times. She was the person I would normally lean on for Big Life Crisis support, but she now was the *one* person I felt like I *couldn't* talk to. Given my travel schedule, I was never home for more than thirty-six to forty-eight hours, so I used what I had become accustomed to as my coping mechanism: I avoided. I didn't slow down the bullet train I was on, I sped it right up. As if running faster away from the shadow at my heels would save me from learning how to coexist with it.

Which meant that for the first time since my teenage years, my mom and I were distant, and we both felt it. A few days after I returned from West Point, I finally spoke with her by phone and it was sorely uneventful. We talked superficially—something we are both allergic to—about my travel schedule, when I'd be home next, what we were doing for the holidays as the temperature drop reminded us that fall had officially arrived. I got off the phone more depressed than before the call.

I have a distinct memory of my in-laws popping over to our house on one of the rare days I was home that season. Normally I could pull it together in the presence of a visitor, especially them since I always wanted to be my shiniest, most impressive self for them. But this time, I just didn't have the strength or the willpower. I sat outside on our back porch crying, still in my pajamas even though it was in the middle of the afternoon. I vaguely remember them waving from afar and me not even getting up to explain my weepy, disheveled appearance. I think our internal Truth has an inherent defiance and can only be silenced and restrained for so long. I was beginning to lose confidence in the strength of the shackles I had placed on mine.

When I finally got up the courage to bring things up with my mom in person, she kept talking about how she didn't understand the "science" of Ancestry.com, as though asking me technical questions I couldn't answer would prolong the inevitable discovery. I said that I was happy to set up a call with Jennifer from Ancestry, who had generously offered to "walk us through everything." My mom agreed to join.

A few days later, the call was scheduled for the three of us: Jennifer, my mom, and me. Unbeknownst to them, Brad would be listening on speaker. He and I were driving—him at the wheel—from the airport to a friend's wedding in California.

"All good, babe, I'm right here. It will be okay," Brad said reassuringly right before I dialed into the conference line. His positivity felt like warm sunshine on a cold, cloudy day.

A few minutes later Jennifer, my mom, and I were all out of

small talk. Clearly Jennifer is the professional ringer they bring in for these very situations, because, damn, she was good.

"Claudia," she said to my mother, "I want to preface this conversation with the fact that there is no shame in what we are about to discuss. Life is messy and complicated, and things happen. That being said, I think we can all agree on the fact that regardless of how Alexis came into this world, we are grateful she is here. So, I'll dive right in . . ." Jennifer said, though her "dive" was a gentle slide into a lukewarm baby pool as opposed to the arctic plunge that the conversation warranted.

Jennifer once again reviewed the "science" involved, as she did on our initial call. "Well, I don't fully understand all of that, but you seem very confident in it, Jennifer," my mom allowed.

"Given there are three fathers between your five children, I can imagine that it's a bit discombobulating to think there might be another player involved and I just wanted to speak to that." Those two words, "another player," hung in the air. I could feel my mom getting angsty on the phone; she was loudly emptying the dishwasher in the background to help keep her nerves at bay.

Looking back, it was one hell of a Hail Mary my mom tried to throw when she said, "Well, I guess that maybe my second eldest's father, who popped in and out during that time, may be Alexis's biological father."

My head was spinning at how casually my mom had suggested another potential biological option. It's as if she was saying, "Well, Mark, your dad, who raised you your entire life, might not be your biological father, but hey, there are two other dads to choose from, so how about this one?"

I think deep down my mom was comfortable with the idea that I could inadvertently share a biological father with another one of my brothers and that would somehow minimize the emotional damage to me, given he was at least someone I knew. It would also conveniently keep the number of fathers between her five children at the comfortable number of three. Jennifer quickly shut down that possibility. "Well, Claudia, we actually reversed engineered Alexis's DNA to triple-check the integrity of our findings and Alexis is not 'whole' siblings with any of her brothers, so the two fathers of your two eldest sons cannot scientifically be plausible as biological fathers for Alexis."

Oh, shit.

My mom was now backed into a corner, and she knew it too. Her stammering betrayed her. "Well, it was, after all, a very long time ago. We're talking thirty-five years, so I'm just trying to remember . . ." She trailed off.

"You're right, Claudia. It can be difficult to remember. That's why our team and I worked to provide you with as many details as possible to help you and Alexis navigate this sensitive and complicated journey. So, if it's helpful to jog your memory, with absolute confidence, I can say that as far as Alexis's biological father goes, what we are looking for is a man who is one hundred percent Mexican."

It was so silent you could have heard a church mouse clear its throat, three states away.

Knowing my dad and my brothers' dads were Caucasian,

there was nowhere else my mom could hide. There was no time left on the clock. In an instant, I could feel the weight and shame and fear engulfing her, that "another player," who was not one of her husbands, was real and evident. I wanted to teleport to her and scoop her up and say that everything was going to be okay, that I didn't care how I came into the world, that I was grateful I was born into her and my dad's arms, and that's all that mattered. This fit the pattern that had existed my whole life: me wanting to rescue her, to protect her, to somehow make her single mom with five kids, working two jobs, and going to night school life easier. But this time, I couldn't be a vessel for her fear, her shame, or her guilt.

Throughout the conversation, Brad and I kept whipping our heads back and forth as if they were on swivels, to stare at each other. After the big reveal, Brad hit Mute and said, "Holy shit, babe, you're Mexican? Fuck, yeah!" I started laughing out loud, the kind of nervous laughter you do at inappropriate times like funerals and right after a doctor shares terrible terminal cancer news. Jennifer piped up: "Hello? Can you hear me? Did I lose you?" she said, trying to invite us to be present in a moment my mom and I both desperately wanted to escape.

I was the first to respond when I unmuted myself.

"Holy shit," I said. "Umm . . . wow. Maybe that's why I've always been so much tanner than my siblings, because I'm actually half Mexican? And maybe that's why my friend Elena, the only *other* half-brown girl in a sea full of white kids, and I were always getting mixed up by our teacher."

My mom ignored my attempt at awkwardness-diffusing

humor and directed her attention to Jennifer. "Well, like I said, it was so long ago so I'll . . . uhh . . . need to . . . umm . . . reread my journals."

Something about the ridiculousness of her response snapped me awake, and with equal parts anger and bewilderment, I said, "Your journals?! Mom, are you fucking kidding me? If you don't mind me asking, how many Mexican men were you sleeping with when you were still technically married to Dad?"

"Alexis!!" she barked. "This is not funny."

"Oh Mom, truuuuust me, I don't think this is funny at all." I suddenly felt the truth of it all beginning to penetrate. My voice started to quiver, matching my now shaking hands. "Brad and I are back in town on Sunday. Why don't you take the time you need to reread whatever journals you can find and then we can talk about who the hell my biological father is when I'm back," I said with tones of both of seriousness and sarcasm.

Tabling things for a few days would allow me to get off the phone with some small semblance of grace. I was grappling with not only introducing a new human into my life story but also acquainting myself with the idea of identifying as part of a new ethnicity. This was a lot to process. I also knew that my mom needed me to give her an out. She knew I was confused, angry, and hurt, and being the source of that for me, I know, felt unbearable for her.

After we hung up, Brad and I sat in silence for a minute. He reached for my hand. I was welling up with tears as I thought about my therapist. "Dr. Carlos was right. It was already too much . . . I can't possibly add this too . . . ," I said, barely above a whisper. Brad looked at me helplessly, wishing he could make it all go away.

We pulled up to the parking lot of the venue. I'm not sure how I did it—maybe practice makes perfect—but I assured Brad that I could put on a brave face and still attend our friends' wedding. It was a gorgeous event, full of love and joy—as it should be. Amazingly, photos of me from that day didn't betray the reality of my emotional state. As I watched the ceremony and as we celebrated into the night, I remember wondering how many people out there were also falling apart, hiding like me behind big smiles and warm hugs. I wondered how much longer I could keep up this whole charade before it all came crashing down.

And then I briefly wondered what a relief it might be if it did.

Which to be clear, is usually the last thing we wonder about when we assume life cannot possibly get any worse. Unfortunately, I didn't notice Life winding up to deliver the knockout blow. I'm not talking about the kind of punch that takes you to your knees and you see a few stars. I'm talking about the kind of knockout that leaves you lying there busted and broken, needing to learn how to walk again, wondering if God exists, and if so, how She could be such a savage, brutal bitch?

Because, unbeknownst to me, *that* punch was still on its way.

CHAPTER FIVE

If you had told me that one day I would be excited to be a mom, I'd probably have given you a confused head tilt, followed by a "Who, me?" and then look over my shoulder, thinking you were talking to someone else.

I just never had that giddy, I've-always-known-that-I-want-to-be-a-mom feeling that so many of my friends have had. The whole concept just felt foreign to me. Anytime I heard someone emphatically say, "Oh yeah, I for *sure* want kids," I'd secretly be thinking, *But how? How do you know you want this huge responsibility that includes a lifelong subscription that can never, ever, ever be canceled no matter what?!* I guess I've been banking on the "Don't worry, when they're *your* kids, you love them no matter what" philosophy.

My dad said he always knew he wanted to be a dad. Brad too. Brad has lived his whole life with an outrageous certainty that one day he would not only be a dad but that he would be an *awesome* dad. He's the guy who, when he meets your kid, doesn't

just say hi and then not-so-subtlety move back to the adult conversation that he was having before the snot-covered kid tried to
offer him a wet macaroni noodle from their mouth. That's me. I
would always rather have stimulating adult conversation without
dribbling, drooling, sticky paw prints on my clothing, face, or
really anywhere close to my personhood. But Brad's the guy
who picks the kid up, then proactively finds a Kleenex and wipes
that tater tot's gross, slimy nose. He's the uncle who intentionally
wanders into his niece's room so she can show him around and
doesn't just take the two minutes I do to be like, "Yeah, cool
Lego set, kid. . . . I'm gonna go back into the living room to chat
with your mom." He's like, "Hell, yeah I want to play dolls with
you, hold your hamster, have you paint my fingernails, and jump
on your trampoline." Then like an *hour* later, shamelessly sweaty,
he rejoins the table of people old enough to do things like drive
and pay taxes.

I envied people who knew they wanted kids as much as people who knew without reservation that they *didn't* want kids. I
just didn't know, period. And for some reason that felt wrong,
like I *should* know one way or the other. If I'm being honest,
Brad's confidence in knowing he'd be good at this enormous
unknowable thing unintentionally made me feel even more
scared that when it came to motherhood, maybe something in
me was broken.

Despite naive fantasies of thinking I'd one day marry Charlie, I had never really sat with the gravitas of that kind of commitment in any real way. It was only after I met Brad that I
could even conceive of marriage as a serious adult decision.

And it was after years of doing life with Brad and the thought of walking down an aisle toward *him* that got me to say yes to being his wife. I never really wanted a dog either, until we spent a weekend "puppy-sitting" a rescue named Gussie, and then I didn't want to be a dog mom to just any fur baby—I wanted to be *her* mom. So no, as a theoretical exercise, I never really imagined being married, owning a dog, or being a mom to a human baby. But over the years, Brad and Gussie clearly changed my thinking on the first two. I now have a deeply entrenched identity as a wife and fur-baby-mama. I can't fathom my life waking up and going to sleep with anyone other than the two of them snuggled in my bed.

When the talk of children came up, I leaned on that experience to assuage the trepidation I associated with being a parent. And truthfully, I relied not just on Brad's confidence in himself as a future father; I believed him when he said that I'd not only be a mom, but an *awesome* mom. If there was anyone I was going to jump off a cliff with, into the unknowable and uncontrollable adventures of parenthood, it was going to be that guy.

Brad and I had been married for several years when our talk of being parents got more serious, so we figured we might as well pull the proverbial goalie. My mom had basically sneezed and gotten pregnant, so I assumed it would be the same for me. Only it wasn't. A year later, still nothing, so trying to get pregnant became an all-out effort. For weeks at a time I would pee on strips to track my ovulation. I stopped drinking alcohol, then caffeine. I went on an all-organic diet. I took prenatal vitamins. I read pregnancy books and blogs. I listened to all the fertility podcasts and TED Talks I could get my hands on. I prayed and meditated. As much as I wanted to work less and stress less, looking back, that was a laughable intention. My work had not slowed down, but instead had exponentially intensified. After a decade and a half of very public, activist-driven entrepreneurism, I had been courted to run for political office. The mandatory lockdowns that accompanied Covid-19 caused me to put the brakes on that political exploration, but my mind and body were still buzzing from the pressures and self-doubt that had accompanied the flirtation.

In desperate pursuit to get pregnant, I also had lots and lots and lots of sex (Brad wasn't mad about that part). Then, because I heard gravity had something to do with uniting sperm and egg, I started doing handstands after sex. You start getting desperate after a while. Months turned into years and still nothing. Yet all around us our loved ones were getting pregnant without a hitch. I did more. I tried harder. And harder and harder. Still nothing.

Every month that passed was a painful reminder of the powerlessness I was experiencing. My identity and my confidence were built on the foundation of the work ethic I'd inherited from my mom, my ability to accomplish and achieve things in the face of insurmountable odds. As an entrepreneur, I had a professional resume of building things, creating things, producing things from thin air. I was a professional at getting shit done.

Now, for the first time in my life, I had found something that no amount of effort or work or sacrifice could make happen. None of my doing, defying, pushing, producing, striving, fighting, forcing, making, praying, or wishing was working. This was completely out of my control. It unglued me. The Superwoman in me had officially found her Kryptonite.

I know life is, in fact, *not* fair. But in one of my less proud, non-PC moments, I remember shouting at Brad, "Even teenage crack whores who don't even want a baby are getting knocked up, so why the hell can't I?" Our fertility challenges were a huge slice of rancid humble pie, and every bite was more revolting than the last.

As we started getting test results back from fertility specialists, I acted tough, like it would be okay because I was never certain I even wanted kids. I went as far as to convince myself that I was actually having them for Brad, because he was the one who wanted to be a dad. I now think it was both impressive and sad that my mind was able to set up such an effective defense mechanism to protect my heart from total evisceration.

We finally reached a point in our fertility journey where IVF was our only path forward, which meant lots of hormone injections, followed by an egg retrieval, after which, any viable eggs would be mixed in a petri dish with Brad's sperm and then an embryo would be inserted into my uterus, in hopes of it taking and us getting pregnant.

I was so afraid of being disappointed after years of trying that I wouldn't allow myself to dream about our IVF actually being successful. I held this idea at arm's length because it felt too dangerous to hold unrealized hope any closer. Then I got the phone call that it had in fact worked. We were pregnant. I was in shock.

There are no words to capture this moment of finally getting the thing we'd wanted and longed for, *for years*. It's so wild how one sentence from our nurse, "Congratulations, Alexis, you're pregnant!" instantly and profoundly changed the entire trajectory of our lives. I didn't know how badly I had wanted a baby, and hadn't allowed myself to even consider it, until it was confirmed that I had one finally growing inside me.

Later, as we were driving home from the doctor's office, I felt that I was finally able to be honest with Brad and more so with myself. I turned to him and said, "I know *you* always wanted to be a dad and that I always joked that I was doing it for *you*, but the truth is, I think I have always wanted to be a mom, it just scared me to admit it. Maybe because I couldn't control it? I hated that I couldn't *make* it happen and the more it didn't happen for us, the farther I pushed it away, because I didn't want to keep being disappointed or disappointing you . . . I was just afraid of wanting something and maybe not getting it. But I really, really *do* want to be a mom. I've never felt so excited about anything in my whole life."

Over the next few weeks, Brad and I came up with creative ways to surprise our parents and tell our siblings the miraculous news. We even found a sneaky way to film their reactions because we wanted to eventually post a montage of our blissful pregnancy reveal. His parents are avid golfers, so we wrote "Baby Buckman 2020" on a golf ball and switched it with one his mom had hit into some rough. When she went to find her ball, she picked it up but didn't really look at it. Brad had to prompt her to read it. She looked down at the ball, up at us, back down at the ball, and with tears welling up in her eyes she screamed, "NO WAY!!! Ahhhhh!!" All the ruckus was clearly confounding for Brad's dad, who finally said, "Damnit Tammy, what the hell does it say?!" She threw him the ball, and he was quickly swept into the same crying lazy river we were all floating in.

My mom had just as wonderful a reaction. We taped a note to Gussie's collar that said "Grandma: I'm gonna be a big sister—Baby Buckman 2020." When she reached down to scratch Gussie, she noticed it, read it silently, and then threw her hands over her face. "Really? Really?" she said as the tears gushed, and she peeked at me through her fingers. We hugged each other tightly, the relief from years of disappointment cementing us together. We told my dad and Jane with handwritten notes on their breakfast taco wrapping, and they too joined in our elation.

Countless people dropped off presents, filling our foyer with boxes and notes saying, "God is good" in response to our fulfilled prayers. My mom brought over the most precious pair of baby slippers with unicorns on them.

"I bought these forever ago and I've kept them hidden until it was time, and apparently that time is now," she sweetly said as she handed them to me.

"Aw, Momma, I loooove them!" Of all the gifts and presents, those slippers were my favorite. I set them on my bedside table so that I was always reminded of this exciting new life chapter. Each morning, as I lay in bed, I'd glide my fingers over the shiny unicorn horn. *Hello baby slippers*, I'd say, and then at nighttime, *Goodnight baby slippers*, before I turned the lights out. Because this is what happens when we are newly in love. We do things that are weird and silly like gush over baby slippers and giggle to ourselves and stay up late daydreaming about what isn't yet but one day will be.

A few weeks later—when I was still in my first trimester—we were with a real estate agent, touring a new home now that we'd need more space to accommodate our growing family. I got a phone call and whispered to Brad that it was our nurse. I didn't think much of it but stepped outside to take the call. We had talked to her a hundred times. In fact, she was the same one who'd shared the glorious news that we were pregnant. I answered the phone expecting the routine blood work results saying everything was on track, as expected.

"Alexis," she said, "we got back the most recent blood results. I'm so sorry, but the results showed that this is no longer a viable pregnancy."

It was as if the whole world went dark in that one moment. No questions, not "Can you explain more?" I just hung up the phone. I stood there in a complete state of shock, the kind of shock that accompanies the deepest, most painful, heartbreaking blindside of your entire life.

The depth of my agony was immediate. It was visceral. It felt like the wind had physically been knocked out of me; I couldn't breathe. I got light-headed. It felt like a meteor had crashed into my world and I'd been knocked to the ground, unconscious and unsure if I was going to survive. Everything I had in my arsenal that had allowed me to sidestep defeat was failing me: my work ethic, my grit, my indefatigable resilience, my otherworldly optimism, my strategic pivoting and creative reinvention. None of it could comfort me as I stared up into the blue sky and closed my eyes with tears running down my face. In that moment, I experienced a level of vulnerability, of hopelessness, powerlessness, and inadequacy that I had worked so hard to avoid my entire life. My heart was beating so fast, my hands were shaking, and my eyes were scanning for an exit through the back fence in order to avoid unraveling in front of the real-estate agent.

I remembered a few years back, when my dad was battling cancer and it wasn't looking good. I was rattling off all the reasons why he was going to be okay, all the reasons why I knew he was going to live. He took my hand and said, "Sweet girl, regardless of whether I live or die, I need you to know one thing: that God is good. No matter what. He is good and His ways are good. Even if we can't understand them. Promise me that you'll choose to believe that, regardless of my outcome." I nodded at the time. But I remember thinking my faith clearly was not as strong as my dad's. My love was so very human and so very conditional. Because if God took my dad, I was certain that I would hate Him forever.

As I walked to the car, all I could feel was the inhumanity of the universe, the savagery and injustice and cruelty of the cosmos, because the wish I didn't even know I had or wanted had been granted, only to, what . . . now be taken away? I couldn't find one iota or flicker of a silver living in all this. It just felt like a deliberate, intentional, blatant betrayal from God. There was no fucking "purpose to my pain." Nothing could soothe the explosive rage erupting inside of me.

Brad saw my reaction to the call through a window in the house. From twenty-five feet away, he knew. He felt the atomic blast of my grief and the same thermal radiation penetrated his body, too. He met me at the car. We drove home in complete silence, holding hands and crying.

There are moments in life in which no words are necessary; in fact they just get in the way. There are moments when touch and tears and wailing and screaming is the only form of communication necessary, when our bodies take over and they contort and snort and rock and shake themselves into a violent frenzy. Brad was my container. He held all of me as I fell apart and broke and exploded and threw things and shouted at the heavens and violently punched the air, rebuking and blaming a heartless, ruthless God who was anything but good.

I was very, very loud. And then suddenly I was silent. Looking back, I can't believe the neighbors didn't come over to see if a murder had taken place. Brad held me and rocked me for hours as I melted into his arms. I asked Brad to share the news with our family and friends. I didn't have the emotional capacity to talk about it. I couldn't add anyone's disappointment to my shoulders. I couldn't function under the weight of my own. I thought about articles I had read about people experiencing such intense heartbreak, that days or weeks later, they simply died from the sorrow. I wondered if my sorrow might do the same. I welcomed it.

In an attempt to emotionally prepare us, our doctor said I would be miscarrying over the next couple of days and while it would not require surgery, it would be a gruesome, tangible reminder of our loss. He was right.

Afterward, I felt like I simply existed in the in-between. I wasn't dead, but I certainly wasn't living. Being awake felt too painful, so sleep was the only place I could find solace, the only place where the truth was blurred out by the blissful nature of unconsciousness.

I didn't leave the house for days. At one point, I woke up in my groggy state and smiled. I think I was still half asleep. I went to touch the unicorn slippers as was my habit the last several weeks, and I violently jerked my hand back as the chilling reality of our loss came flooding back to me. I threw the slippers across the floor and pulled the covers up over my head.

For weeks thereafter, zombie-like, I would crawl out of bed, tie my grubby purple bathrobe tightly around my waist, and walk into the living room. I'd perch myself on the couch and Brad would just sit there with me while I cried. By this point he had exhausted the time he could take off to mourn with me; he had to get back to work. So, he'd kiss my face and say something incredibly sweet and sensitive about how we were going to get through this and then he'd leave.

But I'd just stay, right there in the same spot. Looking back, I don't even know what I did or thought about for all those hours. I was someone who could barely meditate for more than twenty minutes, and suddenly here I was staring at the same place on the same wall for hours at a time, days on end. Barely eating. Barely drinking. Barely talking. Barely existing.

The few times I looked in the mirror, the face that looked back was unrecognizable. My eyes were bloodshot and bloated from all the crying, my face was puffy from too much sleep, and my hair was tangled and messy.

People were calling, but my phone had become a paperweight, an inanimate object on my bedside table. I felt like someone had turned the electricity grid off that fueled my soul's existence. I told Brad I didn't want to see anyone, despite the desire of friends and family wanting to comfort me. My anguish was so excruciating, it felt like death—a place in the darkness that only I could enter and only I could exit. I was in that dark place, where time did not exist and all I wanted to do was dissolve away and feel nothing.

Adding to my heartbreak, the world gave us all a tiny surprise: a new virus outbreak on the other side of the world. People were all glued to their phones scrolling feverishly for updates. As we all now know, in a few short weeks, the entire country would go into pandemic lockdown, and 150 scheduled work events on my calendar for 2020 would go to zero, along with my income. Which is to say: I was now adding a global pandemic and a financial and professional identity crisis on top of my miscarriage, on top of my biological father curveball, on top of already being on the brink of a total fucking meltdown.

One morning, before leaving for work, Brad mentioned receiving a text from one of our best friends, Luke, who was now grieving his own heartbreak and a looming divorce. He said he needed to get out of his house, which had become a painful reminder of his soon-to-be ex-wife. Knowing our situation, he thought we probably needed to get away, too. He suggested a road trip. "What do you think?" Brad asked. I had no reaction, as had become the norm in my semi-catatonic state. Brad kissed me good-bye and I went back to staring at the wall.

Two days later, I was upstairs watching a movie with my mom and Brad, an activity requiring zero energy or effort from me, when we heard obnoxiously loud music coming from outside. So much so that I finally hit Pause and stormed over to the window in a huff to see what in the hell was going on.

To my surprise, it was not an irreverent teenager blasting tunes from his truck, nor was it our polite neighbors throwing a rager on a school night. Instead, it was my best friend, Frannie. She lived ninety minutes away, but here she was standing outside our house, blaring music from her enormous mom-mobile.

"Oh my God?" I said, incredulously.

"What's going on, babe?" my husband asked over his shoulder, staring at a paused screen.

"It's Her. It's FRANNIE!" I didn't really understand what was going on, nor did I really believe that Frannie was truly outside. But a smile had crept onto my face for the first time in weeks, so I was feeling *something*.

Frannie has been my ride-or-die since I was fourteen, and back then we dreamed we'd be neighbors as grown-ups, and that we'd have a tunnel connecting our houses. I wrote about her friendship in my first book about female empowerment. Frannie is empowerment and inspiration personified. Several years ago, Frannie dashed our hopes of having that tunnel when she and her family moved to San Antonio.

Frannie is my *person*; I call her when I want to celebrate, be consoled, am bored, happy, sad, annoyed, need a distraction, advice, and pretty much any other excuse I can think of to hear her voice. She is the person who reminds me that I never need a stage or a microphone or to say anything inspirational or profound for her to love me. Frannie was my first phone call with the news that we were pregnant, and she was the first phone call Brad made when we received the devastating news that we had lost the baby. Other than my mom and Brad, Frannie was the only person I talked to when she called to check on me. Covid had amplified the heartbreak over our miscarriage with not being able to see my loved ones in person, especially when I felt we needed them most.

Without any explanation or warning, this angel in human form was now playing uncomfortably loud music on my front lawn. I went scurrying downstairs in the oversized pajamas that I had been wearing for weeks to see if my best friend had lost her damn mind.

Even with a mask on, I could see her beaming smile coming through her big, beautiful eyes. I hadn't opened my mouth before she yelled from her car, "Six feet, Jones . . . come dance with me!!"

A safe, socially distanced six feet away from my soul sister, with tears streaming down both of our faces, we gyrated and jumped, swayed and danced with our arms in the air as if pulling the heavens down to us was an option. Jamming out to "Can't Stop the Feeling!" by Justin Timberlake, we teleported back to our fourteen-year-old selves, singing and dancing in her bedroom without a care in the world. As the song ended, she turned off the music and breathlessly said, "I know this is hard . . . I know this is the hardest thing you have ever had to go through, Jones, and I know you of all people can do hard things . . . and I just wanted you to know that I love you."

My best friend with four kids had just driven three hours roundtrip, late at night, to dance with me for *one* song, to remind me that she loved me and that I was not alone in my grief. For approximately three minutes, Frannie's infinite love alleviated the deep sadness that surrounded me and allowed me to briefly hear the faint calling of joy.

Her tears spilled over her mask, saying so much more: *That she was sorry. That if she could take my pain away, she would. That it was unfair, and yes, God did have a plan even if I couldn't understand it. That I would get through this, even if it felt like I wanted to stop living. And that she knew exactly, precisely the pain I was going through as she herself had experienced years of infertility.*

She got back in her car, and I yelled, "I love you so much too!" as I watched her drive away. To myself, I whispered, "Thank you sister . . . thank you . . ."

Strange to say, but I felt I'd been sent a sacred sign; Frannie was like a firefly, reminding me that light can still exist in the midst of darkness. Even if the sun didn't resume its place in the skyline of my life that day, I knew I had been gifted the first of many magical flickers. I didn't know it then, but Frannie's remarkable display of love was my first firefly moment. It also marked the starting point of my journey toward becoming human again.

The next morning, I got up, showered, brushed my hair, and dressed in something other than my purple robe.

"Wow, babe, umm . . . you're dressed!" Brad said, slightly too perky and far too surprised for it to not sound like an insult. I didn't even make eye contact. I stared straight ahead, and said dryly, "You know how we always joked about missing the age-appropriate window of experimenting with drugs, and if we did it now in our midthirties, it would just be weird and kinda sad?

"Well, I think we either have to go on that road trip with Luke, so I can get the hell out of this house, or I'm going to start getting real weird, real fast."

Brad didn't skip a beat, "Well then . . ." he said without so much as blinking, "looks like we need to rent an RV, baby. I'll call Luke and tell him we're in."

CHAPTER SIX

With the decision made to get on the road, we got organized quickly. We rented a 38-foot beast of an RV that none of us really knew how to drive, named it Thor, burned a CD of Garth Brooks's greatest hits, and started to talk about an itinerary. We had no real limits on our time line and few required destinations; we were winging this road trip, with no particular order to our stops, no real agenda, and no RV park reservations for that matter. It now being in the middle of a global pandemic, we didn't know if we'd be able to legally cross over *one* state line, much less the seven on our wish list. All we really knew is that we were each committed to about a month of being away and that we would be eating, sleeping, shitting, singing, talking, driving, and living in less than one hundred square feet of one another. We figured it would be an added bonus if we could sneak in a few laughs along the way, considering what Brad and I had just been through and the heartache Luke was feeling as his marriage had officially flatlined.

Gesturing toward the organized piles of everything we'd be packing in the RV, I jokingly interviewed Brad, "Dream trip, what we do we have here, babe?" He took the bait and proceeded narrating while simultaneously pointing out various items, "You got your Yeti cooler, baseball mitts, tennis rackets, yoga mats, weights, ankle weights, wet suit, sleeping bags, towels, you name it. We don't know where we are going yet . . . but wherever it is, we got the stuff to cover it," he said with a big grin. We were clearly prepared for our version of adult summer camp.

It's easy to forget just how big Texas is, with its sprawling hill country and vast planes, especially when you're headed northwest from Austin to New Mexico. Our first leg would be an eleven-hour trip to Santa Fe, where Zeke, one of my brothers, lived.

As we started down our street, I waved good-bye to my mom and brother who had helped us pack up everything that morning. I took a bone-deep breath as we drove away from my state, my city, my street, and my house, escaping my life and leaving behind all my broken parts.

That idea felt liberating, and I smiled broadly at Brad, who was driving. He reached across the armrests and took my hand in his. Not for the first time, I said a quiet word of thanks for having found such a soul mate. And not for the first time, he was jailbreaking me from heartache. Once, several years earlier, he'd come home to find me sitting on the floor of the running shower, sobbing into my hands; earlier that afternoon I'd heard news of a setback in my dad's fight against cancer. Brad took one look at me and walked straight into the shower, without removing a single article of clothing. He didn't say a word. He just bent down, scooped me up into his lap, and sat there holding me as I wept.

I clung to him for a few minutes and then pulled back to look him in the eyes. Water was pouring down our faces like we had been caught outside in a storm. I stated the obvious, "Baby, you got all wet, what were you thinking?" He reached above my head to turn the shower off. "I wasn't. You looked so incredibly sad . . . I guess I just wanted to hold you . . . to take all your pain away."

Looking at him now, behind the steering wheel of the RV, I felt as protected and loved as I'd felt in the shower. Tears of gratitude welled up in my eyes. Then Rachel Platten's "Fight Song" came on the radio, interrupting my sentimental moment, and Brad and I both began belting along at the top of our lungs, arms dancing in lieu of our seat-belted bodies.

As the song ended, my gaze settled on the countryside speeding by my passenger window. I strained to focus on one thing: a street sign, a telephone pole, even something as large as a house or store. But I couldn't make out any details from our speed. It was all just one distorted image after another, all smeared together with no beginning and no end. The blur felt like an apt metaphor for my life. I was living and working at a similar velocity.

That said, until I had started to feel that speed tearing me apart, I had never really considered the idea of slowing down. According to my mom, a full, determined sprint has always been my default setting. "You were never the kind of kid who clung to her mama's skirt or looked away shyly when people were trying to talk to you," she offered. "You were the kid I had to watch like an absolute hawk because if something or someone got your attention, you'd just take off and never look back. You gave me near heart attacks on multiple occasions. I'd look away for two seconds, turn back, and suddenly you were nowhere to be found. You're what us moms called a 'runner'—straight into the ocean, oncoming traffic, off a cliff, or into a lava pit if it had something sparkly you wanted!" she said recently, laughing.

I took a deep breath, painfully aware that for the next eleven hours, the only thing I was responsible for . . . was breathing. Nothing I had to do. Nowhere I had to be. Suddenly, I had *space*, in every direction of the vast Texan horizon. Space to roam, space to drive, and space to think.

The first thought that came to mind was *How did I get here? How exactly did this happen?* I was the woman who had literally written a book on speaking your truth, discovering your passion, and being the most badass version of yourself. And yet I felt so inconceivably far from that in my *own* life.

I exhaled loudly, to which Brad responded, "Hey, what's going on over there?" I smiled back at him, still surprised after all these years at how in tune he was with whatever was rumbling inside of me.

"I guess I'm just really disappointed . . . I've been preaching about self-care and self-love for years and I don't feel like I am any good at it myself."

He took a moment, looked out at the open road, and then

shot back, "Yeah, but don't we teach the stuff we need to learn the most? I remember you said it a few weeks ago. I think you were quoting your girl Gloria." Then, shaking his head with a sarcastic smile, he added, "And you don't think I'm ever paying attention."

With ten and a half uninterrupted hours of thinking time still to go, I leaned into what Brad had pointed out and Gloria Steinem's sage advice. Feeling blessed with the opportunity to disconnect physically and mentally from the world—to just be—I cozied into my captain's chair and let my mind wander. As it so often did, my mind settled on my parents. Here I had the gift of time and the freedom to roam, but at my age my mom had five kids, was working full time, and was buried up to her eyeballs in bills. It was easy to see in hindsight the sacrifices my parents made for us, especially my mom. The sleepless nights, the long work hours, the relentless juggling of spinning plates.

In one of my old journals, written when I was seven, I wrote *I think mom and dad like me best when I shine the most.* So, I made it my business to shine as much as humanly possible, racking up trophies, medals, and A+ report cards. And I was clearly onto something—because despite their demanding work schedules, they always showed up for my shiny, noteworthy accomplishments. When I starred in a play, had a volleyball game, soccer game, or got an award for straight A's, they were there, sitting together in the auditorium or bleachers, their proud, beaming faces giving me the validation I sought. I undoubtedly gravitated to the warm sunshine of their attention. It became a guiding force in how I conducted and eventually defined myself.

But of course, them both working full time (or double time, like my mom) meant that they missed a lot of tiny, unextraordinary moments, too. I came home from school most days to an empty, silent house. I'd pour myself a bowl of cereal, watch some *Saved by the Bell*, and wait. I'd wait for my brothers to come home. I'd wait for my mom to get off work. And I'd wait for the house to fill up with the hustle and bustle that could drown out my noisy, anxious middle school thoughts.

The minute my mom walked into the house from her job as a paralegal, I ran to her and greeted her enthusiastically. She'd always kiss me hello and then often motioned to my brothers that there was a car full of groceries that needed unloading. Then she reached for a wineglass and began uncorking a bottle. Eager to share everything, I'd sit on the kitchen counter and spew forth the details of my day.

Eventually the deluge of my chatter would turn into a trickle, as I'd watch her move on to other orders of business. She'd ask each of my brothers about their uniforms, cleats, shin guards. She'd ask about the time of the next game. She'd nudge each of them to bring her the clothes that needed washing for the next day. She'd holler over the railing to a brother watching TV. He would holler something back that satisfied her line of questioning. Then she'd turn her attention back to me.

"Sorry, honey, what were you saying?" she'd ask while stirring dinner on the stove. Even at that age, I could feel the weight she carried on her shoulders, and the invisible mental bandwidth it took to keep track of and organize so many family details. I didn't want to add to her burden.

"Oh nothing, Momma," I'd say agreeably, longing for time that she simply didn't have to give. After dinner, she'd complete her checklist of making sure we'd eaten, were showered, had finished our homework, and were winding down as she changed for her second job. "I love you more than anything," she'd say as she kissed me. I could smell the sweet wine on her breath and then she'd rush back out the door, clocking back in on the hamster wheel of work to help make ends meet.

My mom didn't drink excessively often but when she did, she was Mother Nature's wrath in its perfect power. She was explosive and loud, breaking things in her quaking fury. And the next morning, like the Hulk transforming back to the timid, gentle Dr. Banner unaware of the chaos and commotion he'd created, my mom would return to the quiet, dormant volcano she once was, shamefully burying the molten lava of generational trauma deep within her. The fear of her explosions certainly kept me on my toes. I became a smoke sign expert, with a watchful eye, always anticipating when she might blow and doing everything in my power to calm the trembling earth beneath my feet.

I unconsciously learned early that anger was not an emotion that could be trusted or controlled, so I'd spend most of my life avoiding and shoving it down for fear I too might blow.

Most nights, I'd lie in bed crying hot tears, angry but not sure at who or why. I lived with my mom, but I also just missed her so much. I hated that she was always working. I had so much I wanted to share with her. More than anything, I yearned for her undivided attention.

This wasn't the first time I had thought about my childhood

and the role my parents played. But sitting idly in Thor's passenger seat watching the world go by on Route 84 was the first time I considered it from a different perspective. That maybe all my running wasn't *toward* something, as I had always assumed. Maybe I'd been sprinting *away* from the loneliness and fear I associated with the non-shiny moments I felt unseen and un-extraordinary?

———

There was no traffic as we headed toward Santa Fe. Covid had left highways and public places looking like eerie, apocalyptic ghost towns. As we entered Fort Sumner, New Mexico, we saw a sign directing tourists to the Billy the Kid Museum, a memorial of sorts to one of the Wild West's most violent and bloody shoot-outs, between Billy the Kid and the Regulators gang. "Oh my god!! Brad, Luke . . . can we please stop there?" I said, interrupting my own deep thoughts.

When my brother Nate and I were kids, we knew every single line from the late-1990s movie about Billy the Kid's life, *Young Guns*. We could reenact all the scenes, including the shoot-outs. Nate always got to play Billy the Kid—the ultimate and beloved underdog—and I inevitably had to choose from a list of nondescript villains.

Tenting my hands in a feigned prayer, I looked at Brad and Luke.

"Pleeeease," I begged, "I just want to take a photo in front of it for Nate. He's going to freak out!"

The boys looked at each other but Luke gave a thumbs-up, so Brad steered to the exit ramp and we rolled up to the museum shortly thereafter. It was closed—of course, Covid—but fortunately there were fake wagons and wooden scenes with face cutouts outside, so the three of us could do our best serious outlaw impressions for the camera, hands positioned like we were holding guns. We looked more like cheesy Charlie's Angels re-enactors than outlaws, but it was the thought that counted.

We climbed back into the RV and I sent the photos to Nate. He texted back quickly and was clearly thrilled to see me reliving our glory days. It was such a small thing—such a short stop—but I felt a little giddy. My definition of adulting was always eye on the prize. Set goals. Accomplish goals. No distractions. No delays. We'd just done something spontaneous and silly and it felt wonderful.

Three hours later, we pulled into our first of many RV campsites. Brad and Luke fumbled around, not yet the experienced pros they would become at connecting our big rig to electricity and sewage. Pulling in well after dark, we had missed any appropriate window for dinner, so my brother Zeke kindly brought us some homemade quesadillas and the four of us sat squished around our little dining table in the belly of the steel beast we were calling home.

Zeke stayed until we were licking our greasy fingers and our eyes were getting heavy. He came back the next day and drove us to a hike—our first of many. Ten minutes in, my slightly out-of-breath brother said, "Whoa . . . why are you rushing? We aren't trying to beat some record; slow down and enjoy it, sister . . ." Zeke wrapped his arm around my shoulders, and I relaxed into him.

A few minutes later, I stopped on the path and looked up. The vibrant green aspens against the electric blue sky took my breath away. I clasped both hands on my chest and took in the spectacular view that was hiding in plain sight. "Right?" my brother said as I slowly inhaled the beauty. I wondered how often I'd missed these tiny, perfect moments in my haste.

Now I intentionally slowed my pace to a steady meandering, pausing to watch beetles march along a log with their armor-plated bodies, shining like nuggets of black gold. At this speed, I could hear the wind singing through the trees and the gurgling of the brook that kept zigging and zagging its way across our path. Another mile in, I stopped in my tracks at the entrance to a meadow. The luscious green with bright-colored pops of electric wildflowers looked as if it were right out of a storybook. There were rays of sun peeking through the tree branches and fluttering leaves, giving off a disco ball effect of light and prismatic color.

"Hey, guys, if y'all want to keep hiking, I'll catch up. I'd really like to just sit over there for a bit," I said as I pointed toward a large stone in the middle of the open space.

"No rush, baby, I'm down to chill for a bit," Brad said.

I didn't know it then, but "no rush" would become the most used phrase in our vocabulary over the next month.

I walked over to the boulder and sat on the moist, grassy ground as my back gently rested against the rock's sun-warmed surface. I picked the closest dandelion and made a wish, blowing tiny seeds into every direction. This slowing down would become a frequent practice for me on the trip. I tried to immerse myself in Mother Nature's staggering beauty, committing to seeing the sun rise and set every day, and vowing to look up at the starry night as often as I could.

Hiking has always been one of my favorite activities. But in recent years I hadn't done much of it because I couldn't justify the time spent on something for which there was nothing to show. I was all about purpose and productivity. And yet, here I was, with no expectations other than to enjoy myself. It felt strange. I felt selfish.

But then Gloria Steinem's words came back to me and I thought, *What if she's right? What if all my inspirational preaching, writing, and posting "for others" was really just a projection of what I needed to hear and learn myself?* The question just seemed to hang there. I didn't feel any pressure to answer it. Maybe I had been teaching self-love and feeling "enough" because it is *precisely* what I struggled with the most.

———

I may have first learned to make a fire at summer camp when I was young, but I really mastered the skill when it became absolutely necessary. That time came calling when I lived on a deserted island in Micronesia for thirty-three days as a contestant on the TV show *Survivor*.

Being on *Survivor* was the hardest physical experience of my life, with countless bug bites, starvation-induced acid reflux, periodically uncontrollable diarrhea, injuries, violent shivering, sleepless nights, and a list of other experiences varying from highly uncomfortable to unbearably painful. A few weeks in, I began to really long for the comforts and luxuries I had taken for granted back home: food, drinkable water, shelter from the rain and sun, a warm shower, a soft bed, and most of all, the people I loved.

The irony is that when I returned home to the creature comforts of the "real world," I often yearned for my time on the island, despite all that I had suffered and endured there. Once my overpacked schedule was back up and humming, I missed the simplicity of an existence where survival was my only concern, a time when my complicated and uncontrollable world had shrunk down to a handful of people hovering around a glowing fire.

There were no mirrors on the island, no way to judge my appearance or obsess over my body's imperfections. There were no screens, no social media, or to-do lists other than, well, survive. No measuring myself by my daily work productivity. No social obligations. No bills to pay. No strict, self-induced schedule I had to maintain. There were no alarm clocks, no bedtime, no gym workouts; there were also no desserts or alcohol testing my willpower or triggering my guilt. There was no family drama, no work drama, no life drama.

Starving and suffering on that island was ironically the most freedom I had experienced as an adult. My only responsibilities were to maintain a fire, boil drinking water, find food, and try not to get voted off the island. It may have been extremely physically taxing, but it was emotionally, mentally, and spiritually liberating to let all the cares of the world, and all the rules I had created for myself, go.

I thought about all this as I assembled the fire outside the RV after that first physically exhausting but spiritually nourishing hike. We settled in, now bundled up in jackets and beanies to protect us as the desert sun went down, the moon took her rightful position in the sky, and the cool of the evening set in. We put away our phones. For the moment we were just eyeballs around a campfire. We ate canned chili, talked, and laughed for hours around the glow. I felt the same kind of freedom I'd experienced on that tiny Micronesian island, though our RV accommodations were far more comfortable than a bug-infested jungle floor.

As the stars began to fill the night sky, I grabbed fixings for s'mores. My mouth started to water as the familiar aroma made me think back to my camp days. The first bite of gooey, crumbly goodness exceeded all expectations. As I went for my second, melted chocolate dripped onto the toe of my right boot. Every day for the next month, I'd see the dribble of chocolate and think about the sweetness of that first night.

Sitting around the fire, with sticky fingers and blankets covering our legs, and in honor of our stop at the Billy the Kid Museum the day before, we watched *Young Guns* on our RV's outdoor TV, hidden beneath a sliding side panel. Even after all these years, I found myself still rooting for Emilio Estevez—aka Billy—to get away from the trigger-happy cowboys chasing him.

I looked around the fire. Luke had fallen asleep. Brad was wide awake, utterly transfixed on this cheesy gunslinger movie for no other reason than he knew how much I loved it. His face was pink from the fire, and while cradling my feet on his lap, he laughed at all the same parts my brother and I had so many years ago, and like me, he cheered for Billy to emerge unscathed.

How long had it been since I'd done something that I loved, with no defined objective or specific purpose? Why had I stopped doing the things that I knew brought me joy? In this moment, I defiantly slowed down. I was completely present. I chose simplicity and space.

I gazed up at the stars, trying to take it all in. Under this magical awning, I started to feel something shift in me. I was still desperately sad about our miscarriage, but this gentle, deliberate relaxation felt so good and so necessary.

With time to reflect, I understood that even with all the tools and directions, I never learned how to assemble all my self-care knowledge in my own life. Somewhere along the way I must have convinced myself that I didn't have the time, maybe even deep down, that I wasn't *worth* the time. With how much of my attention had been myopically focused *externally*, it seemed obvious why my *internal* world had suffered—constantly dismissed, denied, and entirely disregarded.

In trying to examine the *why* behind all of this, I was left with more questions. With all of the "work" I had done publicly, I couldn't help but wonder if the *real* work I was avoiding all along was actually an unseen, inside job? Maybe sitting with my thoughts and offering myself the love I so freely gave to others was in fact the most important work? What if slowing down wasn't selfish or entitled?

So many questions, yes, but I knew one thing for sure: Whatever formula I had been given, whatever checklist I had been handed, whatever script I'd been reading from, and whatever game I had been playing in life up until now . . . *wasn't working.* I needed to find an exit off this superhighway, with a new route and a new destination. The beauty of the stars above me, the majesty of the landscape we'd been taking in, the goofy movie, and the flashback of camp through eating s'mores made it all crystal clear: I was no longer interested in returning to the life I had left behind in Austin.

Later that night, I broke out a new journal. I made a list of all the things I knew I wanted more of, the things that brought me joy. More s'mores, more cold nights outside, more campfires, more warm cheeks, more watching my husband's smile break into a belly laugh. I wanted more looking up, more dandelion wishes, more stars, more unscheduled time, and more talking with people I loved, with no bedtime and no alarm clocks. I wanted more open road and more time to think, to reflect, to process and to take proper, internal inventory. I wanted more space to ask questions, more space for whatever and whoever I was becoming.

In a world that defines us by what we do, in a life where my identity was wrapped up in the martyrdom of my exhaustion and the power of my productivity, joy was showing me there was simply another way of being. And I was willing to follow her anywhere because wherever she was taking me, and whatever it was she was reminding me of, I knew beyond a shadow of a doubt that I wanted to follow her brave, defiant lead. For the first time in a very long time, I felt as rebellious as Billy the Kid.

CHAPTER SEVEN

Per my brother's recommendation, our next stop would be Pagosa Springs, Colorado. As we left Santa Fe, I googled it.

"Okay . . . it says it's home to the world's deepest geothermal hot springs with twenty-four mineral pools varying between ninety and a hundred and fifty degrees, apparently with 'naturally healing superpowers,'" I said to the boys, using actual air quotes.

"It's basically a ton of natural hot tubs along a hillside next to a beautiful, freezing, ice melt river. Looks very *Land Before Time*, with all the heat rising, turning it all spooky and mystical. Not gonna lie, y'all, it feels like the unofficial Disneyland for spiritual people," I said, giggling cynically as I kept scrolling.

Three hours later, I had settled alone into a natural "hot tub" that came with a spectacular view of the glittering San Juan River. Brad and Luke had decided to go off exploring other tubs on the property.

I was half-submerged but Mother Nature had my full attention. With this new, slowed-down cadence taking root in my
body, I took a deep breath and closed my eyes and listened to the
exquisite birdsong around me, and the melody the river played
as it ebbed and flowed around the river rocks.

Google had also told me that these springs were considered
to be a holy place of pilgrimage, that people from around the
world sought out to experience healing. Something about the
word *healing* made me uncomfortable, which is also probably
why it was easier to be sarcastic in describing this place than to
admit that maybe I needed some of those healing vibes myself.

Knowing all of this and sitting in the sacred waters, my
thoughts soon found their way to our recent trauma. Without
any warning, the grief that I thought I had left behind started
to sneak back in. But if I was being honest with myself, as much
as I wanted to blame my heartbreak on our years of infertility
challenges and, specifically, on our recent miscarriage, I knew
my unhappiness could not squarely be placed on a single inci-
dent. I did not break overnight; the cracking and fractures had
begun years before, the fissures sprawling like a spiderweb
across the foundation of my life. It was a combination of the
biological father curveball, Covid canceling both my lucrative
speaking career and my plans for running for office, and gener-
ally being a workaholic with no work in sight. Our losing a baby
was the final straw, just the right amount of stress applied to a
fragile, already compromised glass surface that simply shattered
under the weight of it all. It was everything, breaking all at
once.

I rearranged myself in the tub, arms outstretched along the ledge and my head tilted back on the cement to offset the rising temperatures inside my body. For the next hour I tried to let go of the wave of anxiety and grief that had overcome me. I focused on my breathing and tried to simply exist in that in-between space, not quite awake and not fully asleep.

My thoughts eventually drifted to the conversation I had had with my mom after our initial call with Ancestry. The one in which she finally revealed who my biological father actually was. As requested, she had taken the weekend to reread her journals. We had returned from our friends' wedding. My mom arrived at our house slightly tipsy. Who could blame her? She didn't waste any time, diving right in. "Okay, do you want to know who your biological father is?" She could see the surprised expression on my face after all the denial, faked confusion, and cautious side-stepping she had done on our call with Jennifer. I was fully prepared for more of the same and maybe even "I actually don't know" as her only update.

Without waiting for my reply, she just came out with it.

"His name is Silvano Sanchez." Seeing the confusion, outrage, and fear that cast an immediate shadow over my face, she burst into tears.

"Alexis, I'm so, so sorry for keeping this from you," she said as she took a step toward me. Instinctively, I took a step back, recoiling from the information she'd just shared. I glanced at Brad. His eyes were wide, but his gaping mouth was bigger. Shaking off his amazement, he simply said "Damnnn" under his breath.

My mom broke the silence, sputtering out her confession a few words at a time between sobs. "Just so you know . . . I wasn't a hundred percent sure . . . after years of telling myself . . . that Silvano wasn't . . . your biological father, I think . . . I truly believed . . . that Mark was your dad." She covered her face with her hands, gasping a little for breath.

Even in my stupefaction I couldn't watch my mom in distress and not immediately react. I grabbed both her shoulders and bear-hugged her as she wept.

"Oh God, please don't tell your dad . . . please don't tell your brothers. I don't want anyone to know. I'm so embarrassed," she continued, pleading with her eyes as much as her words. Even though I knew her asking me to keep this huge secret was unfair, I couldn't help but enact a role reversal, hugging and consoling her while I was simultaneously attempting to soothe myself. She had never needed her journals. She had known all along. Anger and empathy were coexisting in my body, and yet deep down I knew her love for me was bigger and deeper than the lie she thought she'd effectively buried.

My mom finally pulled back from our long embrace. She let out a loud, deep breath. She wiped her face and sat down at the kitchen island as though she wanted to reclaim her composure as the mother in this situation.

"I am going to tell you everything, Alexis," she said with a steadiness that suggested she'd rehearsed the line in the mirror countless times before her arrival.

"Your father and I were living in Beaumont, playing on an intermural soccer team which is how we both met and knew

Silvano. Our marriage was beyond repair, we both knew it . . . which to be clear, Alexis, is absolutely no excuse for my behavior," she said emphatically; she needed me to know that she was taking full responsibility for her actions.

I nodded silently as I hung on to every single syllable. "He had the kindest eyes, Silvano. . . . We only slept together that one time," she said, and took a long draw from the cold Blue Moon Brad had set in front of her. She paused, not looking at either of us and cracking a slight smile as she looked off into the distance.

"I had actually scored the winning goal that game. We all went out to the local bar after. Your dad had gone home early, while the rest of us ordered another around, determined to howl at the moon that night." She paused again to take another sip of her beer, then she turned her head to look directly into my eyes; hers were now filling up with tears again.

"Willie Nelson's song 'Always on my Mind' came on the jukebox. Silvano and I made eye contact and without saying a single word, we got up and walked out to his car . . . and that was the only time. He was married, I was married. It was selfish. It was unkind and disrespectful to the people we had both made commitments to and, like I said, there are no excuses. I am ashamed of the choice I made that night," she said unequivocally.

There it was. The simple, straightforward truth of how I was conceived. My biological father was a soccer-playing, tequila-drinking one-night stand that took place at the tail end of a broken marriage, inside a car, outside of a dive bar in a small Texas town.

"But more than anything," she said, her voice now a little husky, "I am so sorry. I never meant to break your heart, honey. One day you will know this firsthand, but as a mom, the thought of your kid hurting is unbearable. And the thought that you are the cause of your kid hurting, well that is an impossible, heart-shattering pain and nothing in the world can take it away," she said with tears streaming down her cheeks.

"But sweetheart, I promised myself that I would be honest and leave nothing out, because you deserve that. While, yes, I am ashamed; I lied to you, to your father, to everyone really and I alone have to live with the consequences of my actions." She took another deep breath, but unlike before, her words were clear, as though she was speaking from the deepest part of her being.

"Alexis," she said as she put her hand tenderly on my cheek, "I want you to really hear me when I say this." She put her other hand on my other cheek, cradling my face as she had done hundreds of times before. "I wouldn't take it back if I could," she said with the most sincere smile, "because here you are . . . my beautiful girl."

My eyes had grown glossy with all this truth-telling, but now I burst into tears. This was such an intimate conversation; I had almost forgotten that Brad was even present. I glanced at him again and realized that he was possibly crying harder than both my mom and I combined. I couldn't help but laugh at his huge heart. My mom followed my gaze and when she saw Brad's sobbing, she let out her first belly laugh of the evening and her hands gently fell from my face.

My giant of a husband joined our laugh attack, wiping his red, puffy eyes. "I'm sorry, I can't help it," he said, choking a little on his emotions and acknowledging that as a silent audience member, he had promptly inserted himself in the scene.

"I know this whole thing is crazy and fucked up—sorry, Momma—you know what I mean. Oh man, I can't even speak right now," he said.

He took a minute to collect his thoughts. "I think my heart just exploded," he said as he put both his hands across the wide expanse of his chest, attempting to comfort himself. Then he started to bawl again.

My mom and I both walked over to him, his seven-foot wingspan tightly pulling us into a sweaty, snotty, weeping hug. We stayed like that for an uncomfortable amount of time before we finally let go of one another and individually tended to our own disheveled selves. It seemed the conversation was over.

But it clearly wasn't.

"Okay, it may be too soon, and there is no rush on any of this, Alexis, but I did find Silvano's son on Facebook if you want to see him." She held her phone out to me, Facebook all teed up.

My eyes grew wide. I hadn't wrapped my head around the fact that I might have other siblings. I grabbed the phone and started scrolling. *Holy shit*, I thought. It was as if I was staring in a mirror. I couldn't believe how much I looked like my half-brother.

"That is Silvano's son, Silvano Sanchez Jr., and he also has a daughter."

"So, I have another brother *and* a sister?" I said incredulously.

Brad's booming voice chimed in, "Oh my god, there is more to this story? Just when I think my heart can't take any more!" He walked behind me and was craning his neck to see the faces I was zooming in on. I was now staring at a photo of my half-brother and half-sister. I figured they were about ten years older than me, with striking black hair and a warmth that permeated the photo. "If you scroll down a few more, there are pictures of your biological father, Silvano Sr.," my mom urged, knowing that was the face I really wanted to see.

A few seconds later and there he was.

"Wow" was all I could manage to get out. Here was where my moon-shaped eyes came from.

"He's really handsome, Momma."

She started to get emotional again. "I'm just so, so, so sorry. I hate that this hurt you in any way and honest to God, while I initially thought it was a possibility, I really wasn't certain. Then by the time you were probably nine years old, I had genuinely convinced myself that your dad was your biological father and I put the whole thing to bed. I guess if you tell yourself anything enough times, it becomes true," she said.

Accepting this truth felt threatening to my very existence. I thought about my dad coaching my soccer team when I was six years old. He was adorned in the same bright pink jerseys we were wearing, running up and down the field with a mob of uncoordinated little girls galloping after a ball. The starkest part of the memory was his unerasable smile as he watched me run, the elation and pride he had as he cheered me on. I had spent a lifetime searching the faces of packed audiences to see that same expression because in his eyes I found the ultimate validation of my ever-elusive enoughness. My dad had unconsciously become the source of my gold stars. And I couldn't fathom a world in which he might look at me differently or choose to not look in my direction at all.

As I soaked in the healing waters of Pagosa Springs, reliving this moment, I thought about the power of our minds and our ability to "mind over matter" even the most seemingly impossible circumstances. I thought about the times in my life that I had ignored my own truth and the fantastical tales I told myself, unconsciously twisting fiction with nonfiction, to justify decisions I had made or not made.

But the memory of that conversation with my mom felt so different. Like the emotional frequency of it had changed. This wasn't a salacious story about a woman's one-night stand at the tail end of a dying marriage. It wasn't a story of a woman shamefully lying in order to protect her own reputation. It felt more like a story about an imperfect woman and her unflinching love for her daughter. My mom hadn't lied just to protect herself. She had jumped on a live grenade, absorbing the explosion and shrapnel of her transgression, to also protect me. She knew the priceless treasure that my dad was as a father, and she wanted a future in which I got to be loved by him.

Soaking in that healing natural pool, I stewed on my identity, who I truly was and could perhaps be.

And then my mind wandered to life's upending questions.

What if I just let go? What if I stopped wasting precious time, energy, and effort anticipating and trying to control the uncontrollable? What if instead, I just let life unfold as it was? Because clearly God was not taking orders from me anyway. That was clear. What a wild and dangerous thought, for a self-defined overachieving ass-kicker to even *consider* relinquishing control. It was a baby step, but a step forward nonetheless.

CHAPTER EIGHT

"It's really annoying how you can find the silver lining in virtually anything," a coworker said to me once with a snarky smile. She wasn't wrong. I was a thoroughbred optimist. Case in point: there was an upside to my deep feeling of "not-enoughness" growing up; it really had become my jet fuel.

Having earned an academic scholarship, I attended UC Santa Barbara my freshman year after high school. But after changing majors, I set my sights on transferring to University of Southern California, because I knew it had one of the best International Relations programs in the country. When the moment came to hear my fate, I sat at my mom's kitchen table holding the sealed envelope with the admissions letter inside. Hands shaking, eyes closed, I took a few deep breaths before mustering up the courage to open it. It wasn't enough to just be "accepted"; I needed to be accepted and offered another significant if not full-ride academic scholarship, as the cost to attend was more than my parents' combined income.

I quickly scanned the letter. Then I read and reread the first line before it finally sank in: "Alexis, Congratulations. You have been accepted to the University of Southern California and due to your excellent academic achievements, we would like to reward you with a scholarship."

I fell to my knees and pressed the letter to my face and sobbed. I sat there on the floor for several minutes staring at the letter thinking that my hard work had earned me a spot at one of the most expensive private schools in the country; *I had made an impossible dream possible.* I couldn't help but wonder—the optimist in me taking over—if my struggling growing up had actually been a *gift*.

I took my dad's marching orders—knock 'em dead—to heart and did what I did best: I kicked ass at USC. At least the only way I knew how to, which sadly, usually implied doing all the things I thought I should be doing, abandoning the things I actually wanted to do. Knowing what I know now, I probably should have been a drama or journalism major. But the serious, self-disciplined, competitive-as-hell little girl was now a well-oiled productivity machine on a mission to impress others, not necessarily to honor her internal tugging. So when my college advisor asked me what kind of fun electives I wanted to add to my schedule—she suggested things such as a 3D art class or improv—I steered her back to my agenda.

"Umm, I'd like to add calculus, if it's an option, not being a math major and all."

She looked puzzled. I tried to explain my logic: "Math is

actually really, really hard for me. I'm more of a word girl, a creative at heart. So that's why I want to take calculus. Honestly, I worked too hard to get into this place to waste my time on classes that don't challenge me." Bear in mind that "challenging myself" was usually a euphemism for punishing myself.

"I see," she said a little incredulously, and proceeded to sign me up for the first of what would become several semesters of painful, unrequired calculus. The deep irony, of course, is that truly challenging myself would have meant taking the classes I actually wanted to take, the classes that actually meant something to me. And improv would have been on that list. It strikes me as perhaps the hardest and most exciting class in the catalog. Truth told, my heart wasn't in calculus; I was fooling myself that taking it was courageous.

Given all I had going on, there were few activities that I would allow myself as a distraction. Hanging out with my girlfriends was one of them. But while we would shoot the shit and talk about all kinds of things—a good distraction for sure—we didn't really go deep, which I longed for. I was used to journaling, self-reflection, and self-examination. I didn't have much free time, so I felt I had to make my time with my college girlfriends really count.

One day, no doubt in a rush to get things accomplished, I sat down with six of my closest girlfriends and announced, "We have a lot of conversations about things that don't matter. We talk about boys and fashion, movies, and sorority drama. All of which are fun, but in the grand scheme of things, don't *really* matter. So, what if once a week we talked about things that *did* matter? Like our hopes, dreams, fears, doubts, and insecurities. Would you be interested, would you come?"

A week later, those six girls did come, and we convened our first meeting in a spare classroom on campus. In preparation, I had written down a few thoughts and a loose conversation guide. It was a bit awkward at first. I shifted in my chair and thanked them for showing up.

"So the whole point of whatever this is," I said as I looked down at my notes, "is to give us a place where we can talk openly about whatever is going on in our lives: the good, the bad, and the ugly . . . I guess," I said, trailing off.

The silence was deafening. We were all staring at our shoes, like we were waiting for someone, anyone, to be brave enough to step up and speak.

After what felt like forever, a woman I'll call Monica said, "Okay, let's do this." She took a deep breath and exhaled. "I've had an eating disorder for three years, and I've never told anyone because it's fucking embarrassing. I keep thinking I have a handle on it, but I'm starting to think maybe I don't." Her bottom lip started to tremble. The six of us looked at her with a combination of embarrassed shock and concern; we'd never noticed this about Monica.

"Shit, Momo, I had no idea," said the girl sitting next to her as she reached out and took her hand. Monica hung her head for a few seconds before someone else chimed in.

"I know what that's like, Monica. I was bullied in middle school for being fat. A year later I was hospitalized because I got down to eighty-seven pounds after deciding to simply stop eating. I'm doing a lot better, but it's really fucking hard. I fight it every day."

Before I could even acknowledge whatever kind of magical and vulnerable sharing was happening, another friend leaned in and offered more: "Obviously my boyfriend and I didn't plan on it, but last semester I got pregnant. When I told him, he insisted that I get an abortion. He said he wasn't ready to be a dad, that it would ruin his life, so I needed to take care of it. I just made an appointment at the local clinic and even though I think it was the right thing to do—because I'm in no position to be a teenage mom, especially with a guy saying I was going to ruin his life— I also kind of hate myself for feeling like I did it for *him*." She burst into tears clasping her hands over her face.

This went on and on. We seven, who thought we knew each other, had all been hiding these unbelievably painful fears, doubts, and insecurities, all the while pretending to be "fine."

We all took turns metaphorically throwing the things that hurt into the center of our little circle. I shared how not having a lot of money growing up and now being at one of the most expensive private schools in the country had made my insecurities go nuclear. While there were certainly tears and hugs and hand holding, there was eventually laughter and smiles, too. For the first time in my life, I wasn't the only container for all the parts of me I couldn't understand, was ashamed of, or didn't know what to do with. I felt profoundly seen by these girls because I was allowing myself to fully show up as who I really was.

Almost three hours into what was supposed to be an

hour-long meeting, we finally stood up and started to gather our things. Monica looked at me and said, "Jones, same time, next week?" The others looked my way for confirmation.

"Umm . . . yeah, of course. If y'all are down?" In unison all six girls chimed in with an emphatic "Yes!"

As much as I was surprised by the attendance for our first meeting, I was astounded by how many young women were standing outside that small classroom just a few weeks later. So much so, I figured there was clearly a miscommunication, and that a lecture hall must have just let out at the same time we were showing up for our unofficial girl club meeting.

I found Monica's eyes in the sea of women I didn't recognize. "What the hell is going on? What are all these people doing?" I said, perplexed.

"Alexis, they are here for you . . . or whatever *this* is that we are doing," she said, sounding as confused as I looked. I was astounded. She just shrugged her shoulders.

"Hello," I said loudly, but it didn't begin to quiet the noisy hallway chattering.

"YOOOO!" my friend Whitney said loudly. She got everyone's startled attention.

"My girl Lex is trying to say something, and this is *her* show, so if you're here for the girl club, raise your hand."

Slowly, like a wave in a football stadium, each girl began raising her hand.

"Oh my God," I whispered to Momo.

"Right?" she said back to me. "We're going to need a bigger room."

Our reputation continued to grow. Over the next few months, we came together as a community of young women listening to one another and supporting one another as best we could. Every now and then while walking through campus, I'd see someone pointing at me and hear them saying "She's *that girl*—the one who runs the girl club on campus." Then I'd get big smiles and high-fives. Clearly, they thought I was cooler than I was; little did they know that back in my apartment, I was proudly rocking a Harry Potter sheet set.

Themes for each weekly meeting were based on what the attendees had requested: goal setting, eating disorders, mental health, sex, finances, meditation and mindfulness, eating better, sexual assault, activism, finding your passion and purpose. You name it, we talked about it. The first half of the meeting, I'd speak briefly about the chosen theme, working off of research notes I'd assembled on a week's notice. Then I'd open it up to the group for wide discussion, or sometimes break up the room into smaller groups so everyone could talk more intimately.

There were a few rules: no talking while someone else was talking, no discussing whatever someone shared in the room outside of this group, and respectful discourse even in the midst of disagreeing. Our tenets were kindness, radical inclusivity, and an open heart and mind to new thoughts and ideas.

I came up with these principles on the fly and printed copies of them at the school library (I didn't have a printer nor could I have afforded the amount of ink required). Each week I'd also try to give out a list of resources—additional reading materials, movies, or documentaries—relevant to that week's topic. After each session I'd ask the girls to leave their comments and suggestions, anonymously if they preferred, in a shoe box I'd carry under my arm as I biked to and from campus.

That box became precious to me because it contained the courageous voices of girls who trusted me to hold their vulnerable stories, comments, and requests. I couldn't wait to get home after our weekly meeting to sit in my room and read all the tender scribblings of brave hearts wanting to be heard.

Years later, when asked about founding the group, which I'd eventually name I AM THAT GIRL, I'd say that I did it for those first brave girls.

But to be honest, I also created it for me. I needed a place that felt like home. On a big, intimidating college campus, that community of young women became home for me, and we became home for one another. They held me as much as I held them. And through their confessions and stories, they gave voices to parts of me that I was still discovering and exploring. All I knew was that up until this point in my life, nothing had felt more aligned with my passion and purpose than creating, growing, and serving this new kind of sisterhood.

I finished out my undergraduate degree as a wolf in sheep's clothing. I was a supernerd by day, sitting front row with multiple-colored highlighters and itchy fingers eager to make flashcards. But when I didn't have my nose in a book, I was prepping for my I AM THAT GIRL group. With my Grandma Bess in the back of my mind, I was forever putting together master plans of how we were going to change the world.

Adding to all this responsibility, I also got a job hosting a show with the USC TV station. I was an entertainment reporter, which meant that several nights a week I'd borrow clothes from friends, get dressed up, and attend movie premieres doing interviews with celebrities on the red carpet. Suddenly this little Cuerni-rat was rubbing elbows with A-listers and dancing at exclusive afterparties, carefully studying and learning the unspoken dynamics of Hollywood politics. I discovered who thought they had the power and who had the real power in each room. I also realized that the people who felt the need to state their power never really had any. I witnessed both the beauty and the beast of the entertainment industry up close and personal.

Life has a way of humbling you when (according to my dad) "you get too big for your britches." I may have been getting invites to Hollywood's biggest parties, but I was still in need of basic housing. I convinced my girlfriend's mom to let me pay her $130 a month to live in her garage. Once we agreed on the price, she handed me a large, plastic garage door clicker as my "key." Halfway through my lease, the garage door broke and would no longer properly close. I often woke up in the middle of the night with a squirrel staring at me from several feet away. I eventually named him Nelson, Nelly for short, and over time, he grew accustomed to me, and braver by the day. At one point, he decided that sleeping at the end of my bed, just past my feet, was a more comfortable option than the great outdoors. Now I had a roommate.

I knew there was a certain irony in me skipping around by day with fancy famous people but living with a squirrel in a garage at night. But all this living among means without means was nothing I hadn't experienced growing up. I figured a real bed was an upgrade from the hammock I slept in at my dad's apartment. Straight out of the "stuff you can't make up" portion of my life, however, I did manage to land myself a new car. I won the Showcase Showdown on *The Price Is Right,* which was filmed right near school and always looking for enthusiastic studio audiences. So, while my parents couldn't afford to buy me a set of wheels, Bob Barker was there to lend a generous hand.

Eventually I soaked up as much glitz and glam as I could stomach, and I knew I needed a new job. I grew really weary of having to ask about someone's outfit—*Who are you wearing tonight?* I wanted to talk about the creative process, and I refused to exploit and sensationalize the private lives of public figures. Asking deeper questions often got me eye rolls from publicists pushing endorsement agendas, but I knew the actors and actresses appreciated the thoughtfulness and variety in conversation.

I didn't need something else to do for something-else-to-do's sake—I had enough on my plate with school and I AM THAT GIRL—but I had my heart set on grad school at USC and, yet again, would need to find a way to afford it. Luckily, three years hosting a red-carpet show had set me up with a pretty hefty Rolodex of connected friends. I thought that maybe sports reporting could be my thing—watching ESPN's top ten highlight reel was what made me and my brothers late for church all through our childhoods, and I could talk sports with the best of 'em. Several calls and a few weeks later, I got a foot in the door and eventually landed a paid gig at Fox Sports. I was thrilled, only now I had to contend with the stereotypes and double standard of being a woman in sports.

My dad commented once, "Joe Shmo gets to forget the name of a QB and no one questions whether he knows it, they trust that he just momentarily forgot. Unfortunately, as a woman, you won't get the same grace. You know the quote about Fred Astaire: 'He was great, but don't forget that Ginger Rogers did everything he did, backwards . . . and in high heels.' Truth is, you gotta know your shit ten times better and be able to deliver it, backwards, in high heels. And I feel sorry for the guy who underestimates my girl," he added with a proud smile.

I spent hours making flashcards and spent countless more hours memorizing them. I had color-coded each sport, grouping them on silver binder rings all stuffed in a gallon-size Ziploc bag that I kept in my backpack at all times. I guess I also took to heart what my momma always said growing up: "Invest in what people can't ever take away from you, what will never diminish. Your beauty is depreciating every second of every day. So, invest in your brain, your hustle, your integrity, and your kindness; they will get you farther than your hair, dimples, and your perky boobs, combined."

I parlayed the relationships I made working at Fox Sports into gracing the set of ESPN's College Game Day and scoring field passes for the 2005 Rose Bowl Championship. For anyone who loved football as much as I did, being on this TV set was the holy grail of the sports world. I had worked so hard to be seen as a girl who really, really knew her stuff and I wasn't going to let the men in sports broadcasting beat me at this game.

Despite my "no problem, I got this" facade, that year almost killed me. I'd convinced my very dubious and increasingly worried-about-me grad school advisor to let me sign up for twice the normal course load, hoping to do a two-year program in one. She bent the rules but made me promise to say "uncle" if I couldn't handle the workload. I didn't even tell her that I had a full-time day job. And I didn't dare tell her I was also ramping things up for I AM THAT GIRL. She was right to be worried: I was hospitalized several times for exhaustion; my body was protesting loudly against the ruthless warp speed with which I lived.

Instead of slowing down, I did the only thing I'd ever known to do; I turned the music up and pressed more firmly on the gas pedal.

———

While I enjoyed working in the entertainment industry, and sports especially, it was always a means to an end to help pay for school. My real passion was for what I was building with I AM THAT GIRL. Something about my grandma saying that I was going to change the world made me feel that anything shy of that would be letting down her and her entire generation. At the time, I felt it not only was my obligation but my sworn duty to do just that.

A week before graduating with my master's, one of my grad school professors gave a persuasive lecture on the influence reality TV has on younger viewers. *Survivor* was at the top of his reality TV list, so that night I watched an episode. I was hooked, not only because the competition was compelling but also because there was an instantaneous public platform created for the contestants after their stint on the show. I put two and two together. I wondered, *What if I went on this show, and leveraged its platform to officially launch I AM THAT GIRL on a national level?*

Assuming this was as easy as ordering takeout, I texted a friend to help me shoot an audition video. Back at my place, two shots of tequila later, we hit Record.

Step one: Make audition tape. Check.

Step two: Find out where Mark Burnett's secret production company is located. When I had looked online, it turned out I was well past the audition deadlines, so I figured my only opportunity was to show up in person and roll the dice. I called a friend who happened to know where the clandestine production offices were. Check.

I walked up to the call box when I arrived at the offices and hit the button. I hadn't given myself any time to think through a strategy. I think I knew that if I gave it too much thought, I'd chicken out and head back to my car.

"Hello, who are you here to see?" asked the guard via intercom.

"Oh . . . hi . . . how are you?" I said, stalling for a few extra seconds.

"Yeah, who are you here to see?" he repeated gruffly.

"Um, I'm here to see Cecilia," I blurted out. Then my inner critic immediately chimed in. *Really, Cecilia? That's the best you got?*

"Okay. One second," he said, and I heard a loud buzz unlocking the gate. *Holy shit. Had that just worked? And who the hell was*

Cecilia? I was probably going to have to explain myself to some sweet girl from accounting.

I walked inside and approached the beautiful woman sitting behind the front desk. "Hi honey," she said. "My name is Cynthia. No one ever gets it right. Who are you here to see, darlin'?"

"Well, I'm here for *Sur- Surv-Survivor,*" I attempted to spit out.

"Remind me of your name," she said as she pulled out a master interview list.

"Umm . . . it's Alexis Jones," I said half above a whisper.

I watched as Cynthia's long graceful finger worked its way down the paper in front of her.

"Hmmm . . . I don't see you on the final forty-eight list," she said, looking a little confused.

"Well, that's weird," I said, tucking that detail away for later use and trying to sound equally confused. "I mean, how could I have known to be here if I wasn't on the interview list?"

"Ain't that the truth, honey. These damn interns are always messing things up. Well, baby, I'm just gonna send you in there during their coffee break if you want to go ahead and head back."

I thanked Cynthia—quite possibly the kindest person in all of show biz, from what I could tell—and walked down the hall as directed. There was no turning back now. I took a deep breath, smiled as big as I could, and waltzed right into the room as though I'd waited my whole life for this moment. There in front of me was a room full of television executives, including the well-known executive producer Mark Burnett.

"Can I help you? Are you bringing more coffee?" one of them asked.

"No, I'm Alexis Jones. I'm one of the lucky final forty-eight here for my final *Survivor* audition."

"You definitely are not," he said as panic officially settled into my bones. "We have taken months to whittle sixty thousand applications down to these forty-eight. We would know if you were one of them," the exec said now rather sternly. Then, talking over my shoulder at the door that was still partly open, he called for backup. "Hello? Can someone please see this young woman out?"

I'm pretty sure this is the part of the story where I blacked out; at least I did so for the next thirty seconds because I don't know where in the Lord Baby Jesus the following came from. I made direct eye contact with the man who had asked me to leave and I said with a level of conviction I have not once been able to replicate:

"Sir, here's the deal. I am an all-American, southern belle Texas tomboy. I grew up with four older brothers. I hiked to the base camp of Mount Everest. I'm not going to cry. I'm not going to quit. I look smoking hot in a bikini. And I just got through your entire security. I think it's in your best interest to cast me."

I had conveniently left out that during my base camp trek, I was in charge of organizing enough food for the ten-day hike. Unfortunately, I'd miscalculated our rations and the last two days all my crew had to eat were dried green peas. Any tracker could have found us by the thirty miles of neon green cow patty shits we left in our wake. I figured that letting my team down was not a good detail to include in my current pitch, so I left it out.

After thirty seconds of silence, Mark Burnett stared at me, turned to the other man, and said, "My god, she's pretty fucking convincing." The rest is *Survivor* history, if you're into it. I was cast for Season 16, the first "Fans vs. Favorites" theme. I left a couple weeks later for Micronesia, the tiny island chain just north of Australia.

To be clear, I was a fan of *Survivor*. I still am. But I went on a reality TV show because having worked in Hollywood, I knew the power of the entertainment industry and the public platform it creates. During press junkets when a reporter would ask, "What was it like eating bats and rats?" I'd redirect and respond with, "Well we all have to sometimes do things we don't want to do, which is one of the many topics we discuss in the community I'm building with I AM THAT GIRL."

Invariably, they would take the bait (maybe some of them were as eager as I'd been to talk about *real,* more meaningful topics) and ask me to tell them more.

"Well, thank you for asking, I'd love to," I'd say as I launched into a well-honed pitch: "We're a badass version of Girl Scouts for young women and we're building communities all over the world."

I wasn't just hoping this would be true; plans for our growth were already under way. I figured that college girls wanting to talk about real things and learning from one another were not unique to USC and I was right. Years later, with the help of my post-*Survivor* media exposure, twenty-three interns working with me out of my apartment, as well as my best friend, six attendees turned into hundreds, which turned into thousands of girls on campuses around the country, and then over a million girls around the world.

I was more than off and running and, as always, busier than I thought possible. I got my master's in one year after all, and then in just over a decade, by the time I was thirty-five—and this makes me breathless just to recount—I had also executive produced an award-winning documentary, had my first book published, starred in another documentary, and been invited to the White House and then to Oprah's house (I'm still not sure which I think was cooler). I had a TEDx talk go viral, founded another company—this time for men (#ProtectHer)—and spoken at places including the United Nations, Harvard, Stanford, West Point, Google, and Nike. I went from thinking I was poor to knowing I was rich. I married the love of my life, bought a beautiful home, trained for triathlons, got ordained so I could officiate my best friend's wedding, and adopted a dog. I traveled, hiked, and backpacked to countless countries, won our country's highest national honor for public service, and was being teed up to run for one of the biggest offices in Texas.

What I was less proud to share and often omitted entirely was how lonely I felt traveling so much; that I frequently struggled to get out of bed because I was so exhausted and I would punish myself with brutal two-a-day workouts when I felt I'd been lazy or had "overeaten." I certainly wasn't posting social media highlights about my abusive self-talk that could become so vicious and so cruel that I'd actually contemplated taking my own life, more than once. No of course not. I didn't share the *truth*: that I was so deathly afraid of not being special that I forever sprinted at warp speed because I'd convinced myself that if I slowed down, I'd be eaten by the monster of mediocrity. These were the parts of me that I shoved into the shadow, conveniently hiding them behind the shinier parts posted about me on Wikipedia.

I was a motherfucking productivity machine on a mission to change the world, the warrior I thought my grandmother had always wanted me to be. That was the only version I ever wanted visible.

The morning of my thirty-sixth birthday, I woke up from a dream. I was hiking in the mountains on a beautiful, warm morning. I couldn't see my grandmother, but I could hear her voice. I kept looking through the sun-streaked trees thinking I'd get a glimpse of her. Then I heard her say as clearly as if she were standing behind me, "Darling, there's more than one way to warrior. . . ."

I shook off the sleep to assess this vivid dream. Here I was killing myself to make her proud, warrioring the only way I knew how. So, what the hell could she possibly mean that there was another way?

CHAPTER NINE

Our next stop would be Vail, Colorado—a half-day drive from Pagosa Springs. Along the way, we stopped to do a short hike and catch a view that friends had said we shouldn't miss. It was summertime at a high altitude, after all, which meant we'd be able to wear shorts and T-shirts, and still take in the snow-capped mountains and aspens shimmering with icicles. The trail was clear and mostly a well-packed red clay, but just off the beaten path, there was snow. Brad and Luke found sticks, packed some snowballs, and played a spontaneous inning of two-man baseball. Maybe it was the weather, maybe it was the thinner air, but I could definitely sense a shift in us all—we were looser, individually and together.

The change was especially noticeable in Luke. When we set off from Austin, his shoulders seemed perma-stooped; everything about his body language said he'd been through hell, that his looming divorce had ripped through his life like a tornado.

And everything he said about the situation made clear how torn he was: he had been betrayed, but he still loved the person who'd betrayed him. Though the details of my final breakup with Charlie certainly differed from Luke's situation, I had once sat where he was now—not knowing what to do with the discombobulating conundrum of loving and loathing someone with equal vigor.

And yet there in Colorado, Luke was coming back alive. He was smiling again and was playful. So playful, in fact, that at one point—much to our amusement—he stripped down to his boxers and made snow angels in a meadow. He was learning to be silly again, to find some joy despite his heartache. I smiled thinking that maybe the healing waters in Pagosa had worked some magic on him as well.

After our hike side trip, we pressed on to Vail and the home of a dear friend, Court. To celebrate our visit, Court pulled out a special bottle of tequila and we drank a liquid appetizer together while waiting for pizzas to be delivered. Court was on a roll, sharing hilarious stories about the good old days and mutual friends. I am a lightweight—especially on an empty stomach—so I pretty quickly transformed into a drunken Giggles McGee. I was laughing so hard that I had to wipe away tears.

After we'd polished off every piece of pizza, Brad, Luke, and I headed back to our RV, Thor, for the night, but I was still buzzed and certainly in the mood to keep the party going. I wanted to dance! Brad and Luke weren't having it, so I started a dance party of one. More stumbling than dancing. I kept doubling over, leaning on the countertop to steady myself in between fits of laughter. I found a big bag of gummy bears and shoved handfuls of them in my mouth at a time. I put together some killer ninja surfer dance moves. All the while, I kept looking over my shoulder at Brad. Not only was he not enticed to dance with me, but he was getting ready for bed and wanted me to do the same. Like a child avoiding an imminent bedtime and trying to appeal to the more lenient parent, I shifted my focus to Luke. Happily, he seemed more entertained and was laughing with me. At least I thought it was *with* me.

Luke egged me on. "Brad is coming for you. You're gonna be busted."

Slurring from the gummy bears and my intoxication, I said "You can't stop a dancer. You can't stop someone who lives for this."

It would take Brad a good thirty minutes to stop this dancer and eventually put her to bed.

I woke up with a pounding headache. As I tried to recall the exact type and amount of alcohol that led to such a rough wakeup, my one-woman dance party started to come into focus. Then my phone pinged. Luke had sent me a text from a few feet away.

"What'd you send me?" I said as I curled up on the couch, determined to sleep for several more hours.

"Oh, you'll see," he said with a devilish grin.

We had spotty reception so at first all I could see was a still frame of me contorting myself into some terrible dance move.

"Oh no," I said, putting my aching head in my hands, already afraid of whatever was about to play.

"You were hilarious last night, babe," Brad piped in. "I kept trying to put you to bed, but you were *not* having it. You couldn't stop dancing and laughing. And I'm pretty sure you ate our entire bag of gummy bears. It was actually pretty impressive. Luke videoed the whole thing."

I held my breath and braced myself for embarrassment. But when the video finally loaded and began to play, an enormous smile spread across my face. I couldn't help but laugh at myself. The girl I was staring at had loosened up, she'd had too much to drink, she was dancing, badly, and . . . having *fun*. I missed this version of me.

I had forgotten what it felt like to let loose, to be—heaven forbid—messy and sloppy and silly. I had spent years polishing my rough edges to slick perfection, making it easier for others to see their own reflection in me, instead of my own. I had become almost robotic, constantly judging myself through a lens of how I thought I was going to be perceived and what I needed to do to protect my perfectly curated image.

I replayed that silly video over and over. I was mesmerized by it. Here was tangible evidence that this wondrous part of me—that I loved and had missed dearly—which had been long buried, was in fact still alive. All I could think was, *When did I become such a people pleaser? When did I start living for everyone else? When did I stop having fun? Was it abrupt, or did it just happen slowly, over time?*

And then I recalled an important moment, perhaps the first time I actively cared what other people thought about me more than what *I* thought about me. I loved performing as a kid—

making up skits, singing at the top of my lungs in the shower, choreographing dances to songs on the radio. In fourth grade, I decided to take those skills to the next level and so I stood up in front of my whole music class to audition for a part in the school's production of *West Side Story*.

When my music teacher started to play the piano, however, stage fright creeped in. I panicked and froze. A kid at the back of the class—Derek Funderbutt—made fun of me, and everyone started laughing. I immediately sat back down at my desk. The teacher admonished Derek and suggested I try again but I insisted that I had changed my mind. I really, really, really didn't want to audition; my face flushed crimson in shame and humiliation. From that day forward I told myself that theater, musicals, singing, and dancing were all stupid. And I decided that I didn't like performing after all. I walked away from something I genuinely loved doing because I was scared that some *Funderbutt* out there would make fun of me again. The seeds of people pleasing had been planted. Like vicious weeds, they infiltrated my internal garden and grew rampant over the next two and a half decades, strangling out the beautiful native plants of authenticity.

A dear friend once told me a story that she heard from her brother, a successful musician. Her brother had a friend who was an undeniable musical talent, more talented than he. A better singer, a better dancer, a better everything. Only his music became too precious to him. And that vulnerability made him too afraid to ever share it, so he never released it into the world.

That story stuck with me. What a shame it was, I always thought, that that boy had let his inner critic silence him. I may have been hungover sitting in that RV, but I was seeing things suddenly very clearly. At some point, I had become that kid. Without knowing it, my career had become too precious. My reputation had become too precious. My entire life had become too precious. I had been people pleasing for so long that I didn't know what my own voice sounded like. I had stopped sharing the real me. Instead, I shared a safe, perfect, and inauthentic version of me that I figured people might prefer.

So, I thought, what would happen if I welcomed *all* the parts that existed inside of me—the sunshine and the shadow, the Zen and the tantrums, the beauty and the warts, the messy and the pristine, the fear and the love, the motivated and the lazy, the chaos and the stillness, the brave and the insecure, the trusting and the controlling, the vulgarity and the refined, the responsible and the unpredictable? Could I somehow unzip the straitjacket of perfectionism I'd been wearing most of my life? And if I accepted the good, the bad, and the hideous parts of me, would I also be more fully understanding and accepting of other people? What a concept. Mind. Blown.

Throughout our road trip, I'd been posting photos and videos on social media in hopes of motivating people to consider chasing their own adventure. But I'd been consistently curating, sharing only the inspiring moments of our trip for my followers. I decided then and there that the real me needed to get up off the bench.

I posted that drunken bad dancing video. My caption read:

"Too much tequila. Mouth full of gummy bears. A solo dance party and a massive laugh attack . . . Basically sums up last night. We cannot take ourselves too seriously or we miss all the fun #JoyHunting"

Obviously, my lifetime of fastidiously protecting my reputation and people pleasing would not be undone in a single act of social media "bravery." But this did feel brave, another baby step forward. I was doing something entirely for me, which was a foreign concept. Maybe, I mused, this small shift in the direction of my sails, the one-degree difference in my metaphorical coordinates, would have the power to drastically change the final destination of wherever I was headed. I threw my phone on the couch and went back to my musings.

I thought about other brave moments in my life. For months after that night of revelation about my mom coming clean, I had tried to honor her request of not telling my dad or my brothers the truth about my biological father. But it felt as if her secret, her lie, and her shame transferred to me. I was tortured over wondering if my dad would still love me. If it would change him? If we would be different? Eventually, these fears started throbbing too intensely, too consistently; I couldn't ignore them anymore. Because secrets, especially those with any residue of shame, grow toxic. I was feeling the effects of the slow poisoning taking a toll.

With the help of my suntanned Santa Claus of a therapist, Dr. Carlos, I realized that the guilt and shame my mom felt about her infidelity was not mine to hold. For months I wrestled with wanting to protect her and also wanting to tear down the invisible wall I now felt existed between my dad and me.

Eventually I approached my mom and told her how the weight of keeping this secret was crushing me. While she was absolutely terrified of the potential fallout, she understood that I needed to prioritize what felt right, especially if it was taking a personal toll. With her blessing, I had made up my mind to come clean with my dad.

The next day I received a panicked phone call from my stepmom telling me that my dad has just had a gruesome work accident, falling off a two-story building during a routine roof inspection. He'd fallen off the ladder backward onto the cement sidewalk below. He was in the ICU and the doctors were unsure if he would survive.

Going thirty miles over the speed limit, my knuckles white from gripping the steering wheel, I ran every red light on my way to the hospital. I was desperate to make it in time to tell my dad the only truth that had or would ever matter, that I loved him from the depths of my soul, and that nothing would or could ever change that.

I figured the reason I had always been so courageous, and flown so close to the sun, was because I knew my family would always be there, waiting to catch me if I fell. A motley crew of imperfect parents and siblings, who loved me with such reckless abandon that it didn't matter if I stumbled, failed, or faceplanted—they'd pick me up, dust me off, and make sure I got saddled up for the next bull ride. My dad was usually the first one to steady me, to tell me how much he loved me, giving me the faith to bravely step back in the arena.

Every day I sat by his side in the ICU as he fought for his life.

And every day, I wondered if he was going to die before I had the chance to tell him the truth. The stakes felt impossibly high when it came to potentially compromising my relationship with him. I couldn't conceive of not having him be the safe place I could land every time I felt like the world was swallowing me whole. Maybe the kindest thing to do was to not say anything at all? If I was going to lose him, how would it serve him to know that my brown eyes were never his? I had finally gathered up the courage to speak my shaky truth, only to now wonder if my truth sharing was actually selfish?

I was ironically sitting with the same dilemma my mom had experienced all the years ago, wondering whether this *truth* benefited anyone but the teller. And here I was for the second time in my life after my dad's miraculous survival of cancer, sitting in a hospital room wondering if today would be the last day I'd get to hold his warm hand.

After thirteen excruciating days living in the unknown, the doctors assured me that this man I loved more than life itself would in fact survive. "Good news," the nurse said to me in the hallway, knowing my dad had broken more than twenty bones, "is that bones actually heal back stronger than they were before. It will take some time. But he'll be okay."

I just wondered if the science was the same when it came to matters of the heart. If I was about to break my daddy's heart with a terrible, painful truth, would it also heal stronger? Would *we* heal stronger? Would he still be the net who caught me when I fell? The source of unconditional love from which all of my bravery was inspired?

I wanted to believe that our love was bigger than a secret. I knew that I had to eventually tell him the truth. And while I thought I had played out every single possibility of how he might react, *nothing* could have possibly prepared me for what was to come.

CHAPTER TEN

As we crossed into Bozeman city limits, Brad and I received a text from a mutual high school friend: "Been following your adventures on social media and saw you're headed to Montana. For what it's worth, Harry lives there now. Y'all should hit him up!"

Though it had been a while since either of us had spoken to Harry, I fired off a text to him. "Hey buddy. It's Alexis Jones and Brad Buckman. We just drove into Bozeman and heard you live here now. Would love to hang if you're around." Harry responded in nanoseconds with the same enthusiasm that he was known for growing up. "What?! That's great news! You and Buck are in town. I'd love to see y'all."

We made last-minute plans to meet up for dinner that night at a resort near Yellowstone. Harry turned out to be exactly as I remembered: a fluffy-haired, side mouth–talking, gregarious sweetheart.

"So y'all are back in Austin?" Harry asked innocuously.

"Yeah, Brad kidnapped me so we're back home," I said, a little less pleasantly. This wasn't the first time I'd made snide comments about where we lived. I loved Austin, of course, but I was not always thrilled with moving around to accommodate Brad's basketball career and now, since he'd retired, his new job that had moved us back to our hometown.

Brad noticed the passive-aggressive edge to my comment and was quick to snap back. "I did not kidnap you, babe, that's ridiculous!" He gave me an *it's not the time, we'll talk about this later* look so I deflected the tension with a softball to Harry.

"The last I heard you were running the dealership in Austin. When did you move here?" I remembered that Harry's dad had married into a car dealership family and that in high school we'd all assumed that Harry would go on to work for and eventually own the family business. I was unclear on how he had found himself so far off the beaten path, living in rural Montana.

Harry explained that he had started out on that path but that after a few years working at the dealership, he shifted from selling cars, which was the part of the job he actually loved, to a managerial position in preparation for eventually overseeing the entire business. That meant twelve-hour days, sitting in an office, staring at a screen. He realized that while his bank account was growing, his happiness was rapidly declining.

Harry came home one day and confessed to his wife that he was miserable and had been for some time. He knew it didn't make sense, especially since by then they had a newborn, but he wanted to quit his job.

"I just couldn't do it anymore. I was a shell of myself and

every morning I dreaded going into work. I couldn't imagine doing it for another month, two years, much less thirty.

"So that was that. Thank *God* for Jess. She agreed that no amount of money was worth me being unhappy. I'd still be working there if not for her.

"We agreed to walk away from it all. Which looking back was *craaaazy*. But look around," he said, alluding to the breathtaking beauty of Montana. "Doesn't look so crazy now!

"I told my parents I appreciated the opportunity, but that I wouldn't be taking over the family business. I cashed out what little ownership I had, rented an RV, and the three of us hit the road. We had no game plan whatsoever. Everyone thought I was nuts, that I'd just walked away from the opportunity of a lifetime. And shit, it probably was the opportunity of a lifetime— for someone else. Just not me. So, we left to find something different, something that was more . . . us."

Sweet Baby Jesus, I thought. Did Harry realize how absurdly courageous and uncommon his decision was? We're taught to choose the bird in the hand, not to leave the comfort we know for the possibility that something different or better, *might* be out there in the bush.

"Wait! Sorry . . . hold up," I said, shaking my head. "Harry, who does that? Who just walks away from that kind of guarantee— a lucrative, stable career especially with a newborn? Where did you find the audacity to take such a leap of faith?"

That's when his voice got husky and he leaned in like he was telling us a deep secret. Instinctively, Brad and I leaned in closer too.

"Well, this is going to sound kind of cheesy. But I heard this guy once say that whenever you're trying to discover your passion or find it if it has gone missing, one trick is to just look at your coffee table. Because the magazines and picture books lying there are probably highlighting the things that bring you joy . . . and that is your answer. So, no exaggeration, I went home and did just that. Our coffee table was filled with food magazines and travel books. After all, Jess and I did meet in culinary school; and all we ever did was daydream about integrating our love for food with our love for adventure and our expertise in hospitality. And I was willing to give up everything we *had*, for what we actually *wanted*." He leaned back and smiled.

That phrase started ricocheting back and forth inside my head like a pinball. *Giving up everything you have, to get what you actually want.* Undoubtedly, I'd be circling and asterisking that phrase when I journaled later that night.

Harry continued, "Long story *longer* . . . we came to Bozeman for a random Fourth of July weekend and fell in love. I started looking around and found an RV park that was for sale near here. We thought, what the hell? What we don't know, we'll learn. For the past several years we've been running that little RV park May through October. Then we shut it down around Halloween, lock the gates, and rent Airbnbs for a few weeks in cities around the world, hitting up the locals for the best food recommendations. Hospitality, travel, food—it's a life perfectly tailored to us," he said with a rare, earned confidence.

"Wow," I said. "Just wow. What an amazing life you and Jess have created for your family, Harry."

The three of us talked a few more hours, until they had to practically kick us out. We walked outside into the cold, windy Montana air and hugged Harry good-bye. Brad and I got into our rental car. We were quiet at first. I broke the silence. "I honestly can't believe Harry moved to Montana?!" I laughed with both disbelief and envy.

"I mean . . . amazing for *him*, but that's not . . . like . . . an option for *us*, right?" I said tentatively.

"No, of course not, babe, that'd be crazy. Our family, our jobs, our entire lives are in Austin."

"Yeah, no . . . of course, I know. You're right." I shook my head in agreement but wasn't sure I did. Harry had officially shown me a key to a world that I didn't even know existed.

The last thought I had before I fell asleep that night was *Fuck a bird in the hand. I want the two in the bush!*

CHAPTER ELEVEN

In fourth grade our class did one of those "professional predictor/personality tests." I eagerly answered all the questions, excited to learn of my destiny. Clearly, I had missed the memo that this was just a fun classroom exercise. Instead, I felt like the gods were speaking and my future would soon be set in stone.

The official results offered not one, but *three* shiny options. That night, I wrote about them in my journal.

I am going to be a politician, a preacher, or a TV host. And I know this because Mrs. Harris's test told me so today. I like to talk and my mouth will make me rich. Unless I'm a preacher because I don't think loving god makes you rich. Anyhoo that's the update for today. Thanks.

Fourteen years after I'd taken Mrs. Harris's test, I could check off two out of three of its predictions. I'd been a TV host with my red-carpet gig and sports reporting. And shortly after getting my master's degree, I became a paid speaker, "preaching," albeit not in the traditional sense.

While I had always been passionate about potentially running for public office one day, that day was presenting itself exponentially sooner than I had imagined. Certainly, public service felt like a natural evolution from a career steeped in activism, but when I was approached by the "powers that be" in Texas politics, it felt humbling, exhilarating, and terrifying.

When I told Brad I had been approached, I was a little tentative. I knew that his life would be upended if I threw my hat in the ring.

"Well, I'm not surprised. That was always the game plan, right?" Brad playfully added, "Ohhh . . . you thought I married you because I loved you?! No way, you're just a means to an end, to get the golden ticket so I can become the country's first gentleman." He laughed and pulled me in, kissing my neck until I squealed.

"Brad, I'm serious . . . what do you think?"

He took a deep breath. "I'm serious too. You asking me what I think about all of this feels a bit silly. This is what I signed up for, honey. I never thought I'd have you all to myself, I knew I'd always be sharing you with the world. If politics is the arena where you think you can make the most positive impact, so be it. I'm in, one hundred and ten percent."

I must have just stared at him, because he elbowed me and said, "Honey, you're doing that thing . . . where you're just awkwardly staring at me, thinking thoughts, and it's creepy." I laughed and leaned in and squeezed him tightly.

Internally I wasn't as sure as Brad—was this really the arena where I could have the greatest impact? Could I be 110 percent sure too? We agreed that I would take more exploratory meetings to see where, if at all, I could make a positive difference in Texas politics.

Over the next few months, I was contacted by several politically influential Texans, each informally inquiring about my willingness to explore running for office. Then an absolute all-star team of political operatives at the national level pegged me as a person who could star in the ultimate underdog story. When it was first proposed to me by the head of the team, my response was, "Governor?" almost spitting my sandwich out. "You're fucking kidding, right? That's absurd!"

"Why? Why not you?" he asked.

"How can I even begin to answer that question?" I said, still thinking this was some kind of joke. The team was supposed to identify a race they felt was winnable in the next two to three years.

"OH MY GOD, you aren't kidding? I thought we were starting small, like state senate or school board, something reasonable."

"But you aren't reasonable," he shot back.

He then did what he does best: win over potential candidates. "Normal people hike reasonable mountains; you fly to Tibet to hike the base camp of Mount fucking Everest . . . and you hiked a hundred of the hundred and fifty miles on a broken hip I might add. Normal people get a job working for an existing company and a reliable paycheck; you start your own, around activism, and gain a million passionate followers. Most normal people don't give a damn and they color inside the lines. You give more damns than anyone I have ever met. You stand up for what you believe in. You don't run away when you get scared. You get bigger, you dig your heels in deeper, you stand your ground and you fight. You don't accept status quo, you are crazy enough to believe that things *can* change and *get* better, that we, flawed-as-shit humans, can *be* better. So no, Alexis, you are not *normal*. You fucking care about your people and strangers, equally. You love harder than anyone I've ever met. Your faith is bigger and more real to you than all the hate and cruelty in this world and *that* is who we need running for office. So why not you?"

"Whoa . . ." I said, a bit shell-shocked by his whole passionate speech. "Did you memorize all those bullets or was that actually off the cuff?"

"Well, both . . . kind of," he said. "So, how'd I do?" he said.

I spoke slowly. "I don't disagree that I care a lot, that I love hard, and that I am crazy enough to believe that things can actually change for the better . . . but I always thought that running for office would be decades in the future."

What went unsaid were all my fears: that people would think I was too young, too unexperienced, and that even if I came across as tough, I was deeply sensitive and I was afraid the mean-spirited nature of politics might eat my soul or make me lose all that faith in humanity that he was espousing I had. As much as I wanted to speak truth to power, I didn't want to be a late-night TV punch line or get death threats on the regular. What I wanted to say was it scared the shit out of me to put my life on any more display than it already was, knowing it was guaranteed that half the country would immediately hate me just based on what jersey I chose to wear.

He interrupted my internal dialogue. "As you know, in Texas, the governor appoints fifteen hundred positions across the state. *This* is why we want you to run for this particular position, and why we think you could actually win; because we believe that no one can raise more money than you, that you are qualified for this position, and that you'd change the face quite literally of this state by getting to *appoint* fifteen hundred new, passionate, diverse leaders. So, again, I ask, why not you?"

He was right about one thing. I was not a reasonable person. I never had been. So, it was inauthentic for me to take a reasonable path to any destination. No doubt I was honored to be asked to consider the opportunity. I was overwhelmed by the belief others had in me. They were willing to quit their jobs to support this outrageously inspiring idea; it felt selfish to question it. I loved the idea of disrupting an antiquated system and inspiring young people to participate and believe in the leadership of our state, much less country, again. And the race was a few years out—I assured myself that I had time to get my bearings, to want this 110 percent. And so, I said yes to more *exploring* this great adventure.

A few months later, I met with a cohort of professional strategists, fundraisers, and policy experts. I was sitting among them, trying to keep up with the conversation they were having about me.

"She will have to announce by this time," one person said.

"Her policy team will have to prep her on the latest findings about this," said another.

"Brad will have to be prepped for this," said a third.

Suddenly, I felt uneasy, a physical discomfort in response to thoughts I couldn't push away any longer. Put plainly, I was starting to have reservations about running, and the doubt felt unnerving. Of course, I knew that I had voluntarily boarded this train. I set the destination. And I invited many people I loved and respected to come along with me. Only at some point, I became unsure of the destination. I wasn't certain it was actually *my* dream or if it was the echoes of a fifth-grade girl thinking she was living out a life she had been told—by a silly personality test—she was *supposed* to live.

On the flip side, another voice in my head argued, *This is your dream. This is what you have worked for your entire life. If you walk away now, you are walking away from the opportunity of a lifetime and all these people will be disappointed that you wasted their time and their money. So, by God, get up off the floor of your pity party, wipe your tears, and put that smile on your face, because you want this!*

I looked at that group of people I was terrified to disappoint, and I hid all my fears, insecurities, and doubts behind a smile the size of Texas.

The irony was that I was getting credit and validation for being heroic enough to throw my hat in the ring and run for office, but what I was doing wasn't courageous at all. Brave would have been interrupting the meeting to say how unimaginably grateful I was but that I was actually having reservations about running for office. That at this particular point in my life, running might not be the best option for me and the family I wanted to build.

Brave would have been saying that it ironically felt less scary to sign myself up for an impossible political race than to face the reality of my infertility; that running for governor was probably just a really good distraction from all that personal heartbreak and disappointment I was running from.

Brave would have been prioritizing my health, my heart, and my life above the expectations of others; admitting that I was actually exhausted, burned out, in need of a break to rest and recharge from *years* of not taking care of myself.

Brave would have been giving voice to all those fears, acknowledging them, working through them, and being honest about their existence.

I was not brave that day.

I had obviously mentioned our "fertility situation" to my political team. We had figured out a time line where my "having a baby"—discussed like a dental procedure to be scheduled—wouldn't interfere too much. Unfortunately, my test results stated that the odds of me getting pregnant naturally were slim to none. And I hated it. I hated it on a cellular level, someone telling me that something was fundamentally wrong with my body and my baby-making capabilities were broken.

I had absolutely no clue how I was going to build out my

entire campaign, magically get pregnant at the scheduled time, announce that I was running for office, have a baby, and get back on the campaign trail while nursing in the sprinter van in between stump speeches. But chasing external validation was something I had done my entire life, and it had long been proven to be an incredibly effective way to avoid shadowboxing with my deepest feelings of inadequacy. Lord knows, I'd do anything to not get in *that* ring. So, I just kept going, and going and going, not skipping a beat. Political fundraising phone calls, strategy sessions, medical exams, blood samples, working out, eating, sleeping, repeating.

During one of these many uncomfortable procedures, my doctor was trying to talk to me about what the vaginal ultrasound was showing him on a blurry black and white monitor. "Unfortunately, Alexis, you have cysts here, so . . ." he began. But I was busy multitasking. With my legs spread wide open on the exam table, I was on my cell phone, trying to close a campaign donation to meet my fundraising goal for the day. As politely as I could, I put my finger over my mouth to quietly shush him. This was the epitome of my life, shushing anyone and anything, myself very much included, that reminded me of the lack of control and powerlessness I felt when it came to motherhood.

Later that week, I crawled into bed with Brad. He took my hand in both of his and held it on his chest.

"Baby," he said, "I love you so much and I'm so proud of you and I know you can literally do anything."

After a brief pause, he went on. "I just want to make sure you really want to do this because I'm seeing you razzle and dazzle people . . . like you're fucking intoxicating to watch in action . . . but I'm just afraid that when I look at your eyes, honey, it's kind of like you aren't really there, like there's . . . no light anymore."

A huge lump was beginning to form in my throat.

He continued despite my silence. "And . . . well . . . if for any reason, it's okay if you don't want to run for office . . . with everything going on . . . with us trying to get pregnant . . . I just want to make sure you love what you do and I'm starting to think you may not really want this . . . or maybe, just not right now."

I had been praying for a divine intervention and there he was. An unlatched window, the arm reaching in to save me from myself was Brad's. But instead of climbing out of the window toward the escape I had been asking for, I slapped his hand away, locked the window, and marched on in the direction of where I knew I didn't want to go . . . to chase a dream I no longer wanted to chase.

I did what I always do when I'm scared. I doubled down.

"Of course I *want* this, Bradley." I only say his full name when I'm angry or intentionally being patronizing. "Are you kidding me? This is my life's dream, so . . . I don't know why you'd say that or think that I don't want this. I have light in my eyes. Like, so much . . . light. And who says 'razzle dazzle'? You should think about that." I rolled over and went to sleep.

CHAPTER TWELVE

I recently discovered that my name, Alexis, means "protector of humanity." I know. No pressure. I always thought I was put on the planet to protect girls and women, until I stood in a room full of men.

Yogi Roth, the USC quarterback coach who later went on to be a top sports broadcaster, was and still is one of my best friends from grad school. He knew all about my work with I AM THAT GIRL but when he called me late one night several years after I'd launched it, he wanted to know if I'd expand my reach.

"Jones," he said, "I know you love working with women. But I was curious if you'd consider letting me fly you to Portland so you could speak at Elite 11 on the importance of respecting women?"

Elite 11 was the most prestigious quarterback competition for high school athletes in the country. It would take place at Nike headquarters and would be filmed as a documentary for ESPN. The attending young men regularly go on to start for D1

teams, are drafted into the NFL, and eventually become house-
hold names and Super Bowl champions. Would I speak to these
guys about respecting women and about what kind of leaders
they could be on and off the field? No question. I agreed to Yogi's offer without hesitation. I later found out that in the history
of the program, I was the first woman ever invited to speak. And
it would be a first for me too—the first time I'd ever spoken to an
all-male audience.

Given Brad's lifetime spent in locker rooms, I immediately
asked for his advice. I knew he'd likely been given this same talk
in high school, college, and various professional locker rooms,
and I wanted to know what had resonated. Brad asked if I knew
who would be attending in advance.

"Yes, I have a list of the guys. Top high school quarterbacks,
past and present NFL players, and top executives from Nike and
ESPN. Why?"

Brad chose his words carefully. "Well, as athletes we've heard
this talk a thousand times from coaches and sometimes officers
coming in telling us the ramifications of our actions if we hurt
or assault a woman, but I've never heard it from a *woman's* perspective. And to be honest, most guys don't think this conversation applies to them because they believe they would never
intentionally hurt a woman. Or they immediately feel shamed,
like they have already done something wrong just for being a
guy, so they zone out. But I think it would be different if they
think you're talking about someone they actually know and love.
So, if I were you, I'd pull pictures of their sisters, moms, and
girlfriends and put them in your presentation."

I thought about it and said, "Not gonna lie, a bunch of guys walking into a presentation with a stranger who has photos of their loved ones starting back at them feels super sketchy, but honestly, I love the idea."

Over the next few hours, I scrolled through social media and pulled as many personal photos from holidays, birthday parties, anniversaries, and family vacations from the lives of men on the list of attendees, a group of young men, professional athletes, and male executives I had never met.

After Tent Dilfer, a Super Bowl–winning quarterback and ESPN commentator, introduced me, I started with a bang.

"In addition to loving and being loved by exceptional men, I have also spent a decade speaking to girls and women all over the country about their unique challenges and the societal pressures they face." I could see eyes already starting to glaze over as I rattled off nameless, faceless statistics while pointing to graphs and charts on the screen behind me.

Then I clicked to the next slide. And the next.

"But it's different when it's *her*, right?" They were now staring at a series of faces of girls and women they knew personally and loved dearly.

The energy of the room changed. Glazed eyes and slouched posture were replaced with crystal-clear focus and straight backs.

"It's different when it's your sister, Maya. Your daughter, Maddie. Your girlfriend, Victoria. Your niece, Addy. Or your mother, Devorah." I had memorized the names of these girls and women. I spoke slowly and methodically as I clicked each slide. By the time I finished, you could hear a pin drop. Just like

Brad had expected, I now had their full, undivided attention. Personalizing the conversation had changed *everything*. The energy was now electric.

I was not lecturing, shaming, or blaming; I was inviting all these boys and men to imagine someone they loved in the place of a theoretical stranger. I celebrated the incredible men doing it *right* and talked about how we needed real-life superheroes. I told them that we needed brave men not just helping to change college campus culture and "locker room talk," but warriors who would help redefine how we better respect, honor, and protect all people.

The next morning Yogs texted me and asked me to call him right away; he had to tell me a hilarious story, he said.

Yogi proceeded to tell me that the next day all the guys woke up, headed to breakfast and straight to their first session of drills. While they were warming up, they apparently kept asking the coaches where "Columbus" was and if she was coming back.

"Who are you talking about?" Yogi asked one of them.

"'That girl' who spoke to us yesterday."

"You mean Alexis Jones? No, she's not coming back. She flew out after the talk. But real quick, why are y'all calling her 'Columbus'?" Yogs asked.

As Yogi relayed it to me, the QB got a huge grin on his face and said, "Yo, coach, cuz she showed us a world we didn't know existed."

I had no idea that saying yes to Yogi would change the trajectory of my professional life in a matter of weeks. A video clip of the event went viral. My speaking agents called saying they couldn't answer the phones fast enough. I'd spend the next five years speaking in the most prestigious locker rooms in the country. During this time, the #MeToo movement would find its footing, so then the invitations started coming from Fortune One Hundred companies, the White House, Oscar Award–winning actors, prisons, the military and military academies—all asking me to speak, to provide content, to consult. ProtectHer, my digital education company, was born.

I was asked in an interview about where my inspiration came from in building ProtectHer. My answer was simple: I have a philosophy that men are not simply the problem. They are also an integral part of the cure. I was born into my dad's arms. I married Brad. I have amazing brothers, male friends, and male mentors. I am a connoisseur of phenomenal men because I have been raised by them, loved by them, guided by them, and protected by them my entire life. And while there will always be bad apples, I believe the good men out there significantly and exponentially outweigh the bad ones.

CHAPTER THIRTEEN

In the wake of my father's amazing remission from lymphoma and multiple myeloma, I happened to be present when a nurse asked him about how he maintained his strength and faith during months of painful treatments all the time, with very low chances of survival.

"What do you think kept you going?" she wondered.

Even on my dad's worst and weakest days, he never forgot a doctor or nurse's name. Today was no different. "Well, Rosie," he said, "I just looked at it like this . . . I have one job . . ." Rosie interrupted. "That's right," she said, "you've worked at the University of Texas for well over thirty years . . ."

My dad responded to her hypothesis, "Very true, but not the job I was referencing. Like I said, I have one job . . . and that's walking her down the aisle." He pointed over at me.

Both the nurse and I wiped tears from our eyes.

I couldn't help but think about that conversation and how

much my dad loved me as I walked into the rehabilitation hospital. After his brutal work accident, basically doing a backflip off a two-story building and actually surviving, he had finally been released to another facility, where he'd stay for the next several weeks doing intense physical therapy. Though it would certainly be painful, I was assured he would make a full recovery.

I wrote and rewrote a letter to my dad countless times before I finally printed it out in fourteen-point Comic Sans font. It was a complete confession of the truth, from the Ancestry call to Mom's confirmation to the identity of my biological father. I folded it neatly into my purse, without an envelope, which for some reason made it feel too formal.

Knowing my dad actually knew Silvano, I shared his full name. I told him how scared I was to tell the truth. I told him I prayed that our love and our family's love was bigger than this single data point of my conception. I hoped that he would feel the same way.

My dad sat up and greeted me with a big smile as I walked into his room. I'm sure he assumed I was popping in for one of my regular daily visits. I attempted to smile back as I slid my hand into my oversized purse, blindly searching for the folded piece of paper. My face was trying to maintain an expression of "nothing to see here" while I could already feel my heart rate escalating and my fingers trembling.

I thought I'd be brave enough to read the letter to him; at least that was my intention. Instead, I panicked. I awkwardly thrust the letter into his lap and managed to aggressively say, "I love you and I'm sorry, I have to go" as I ran out of the room. I could only imagine what he was thinking. By anyone's standards it was, at best, incredibly strange behavior.

By the time I reached my car, I was sweating and breathing heavily. I fumbled with the phone trying to call Brad. When he answered, I blurted out, "What have I just done? I ruined everything. I just threw a grenade into my family because I'm selfish, my dad is going to disown me, and my mom's worst fears are going to come true that my dad and stepmom are going to hate her and now we can't do all our holidays together like we always do as the wonderfully functioning, dysfunctional family that we are."

Brad responded gently, "Baby, what are you talking about?"

"The letter! I was going to read it to him, but I freaked out and I just handed it to him and now I wish I could go back in and take it back but what if he's already read it. Oh God, do you think he has? Why hasn't he called me. I bet he's mad. Heartbroken. Shit. What did I just do?" I said desperately.

"All you did was tell the truth, honey. I know it wasn't easy. But I'm proud of you," Brad said calmly.

"And I believe it's all going to work out."

I appreciated the support, but this time I didn't want Brad's sunshine. This was a cloudy fucking day. I wanted him to sit with me in the chaos and fear and feel all the terror that had turned the blue skies in my life into an ominous black. I wanted him to say, "If you feel like the sky is falling, well, honey, then I too feel like the sky is falling," not this *don't worry, the sun will come out tomorrow* bullshit.

I drove home, crawled into bed, and pulled the covers over

my head. It was the middle of the day, so I knew I wasn't going to fall asleep; I just needed to escape. I was in an emotional free fall, trying to drown out the voice inside that was taunting me with thoughts like *Told you you'd break your dad's heart . . . He probably doesn't love you anymore . . . You're such a selfish girl . . . You should have kept your mouth shut.*

After several hours of this anguish, I called my stepmom's cell.

"Honey, are you okay?" she said when she could hear the tears in my voice.

"Well," I said a little croakily, "it's just that I wrote Dad a letter." I hoped she'd take the cue and give me some idea as to how he'd taken it.

"Okay . . . and?" she said, clearly having no idea what I was referring to.

"Well . . . in the letter I said some things and was just curious if Dad had read it."

"Oh, I'm here with him, let me just ask," she said.

I swallowed hard.

"Mark . . . Mark, it's Alexis. She's asking about a letter she brought by. She wants to know if you've read it."

Though he answered her right away, it felt like a lifetime. I couldn't breathe; I felt like I had a mouth full of hot sand and it was burning the back of my throat.

"Oh shoot. Tell her sorry. Haven't had a chance to yet. Does she need me to read it now? It's just that the game is still on."

I couldn't help but smile. I had worked myself into a complete emotional frenzy and my dad hadn't so much as read the damn thing. Jane's voice came loudly back on the phone to relay the message I had just heard myself.

"Sorry, sweetie, apparently he hasn't read it yet. Do ya need him to read it now?"

"It's okay. Please just tell him to read it when the game is over. Please tell Dad I love him." I hung up relieved—temporarily—and exhausted. I'd run twenty marathons in my head.

A few hours later, I was finishing up dinner with a friend. I reached for my phone and saw I had a single voicemail, from my dad.

"Hi sweet girl, it's me. I uhh . . . I read your letter. And . . . can you come over first thing tomorrow morning? There's something else I want to talk to you about. . . . Umm . . . I love you." I replayed it over and over. I smiled every time he said "I love you." I slept well knowing he could still say those three words to me. But what *else* could he want to talk about?

Early that next morning, I walked into my dad's rehab room.

"Ol' Silvano Sanchez, huh?" he said with a sarcastic grin. No warmup, no small talk.

In the next twenty seconds, my worst fears were played out inside my head like a nightmare: My dad, unable to look me in the eye, his mouth quivering, said, "I'm sorry, I just don't know what to say, but . . . you're not my daughter. I know it's not your fault, but I just can't deal with this. Please, I just need you to leave . . ." And then I leaned in to hug him and he went stiff as he coldly pulled away, clearly ashamed of me. I watched myself as I ran through the hallway to the safety of my car, unable to breathe, unable to think, unable to imagine a life where his love and his touch were eternally revoked. I couldn't wrap my head around a world in which my daddy chose to no longer love me and how I could or would ever recover from losing him.

Thankfully my dad interrupted the horror movie I was silently playing in my mind and didn't wait for me to respond to his initial question. "There are two things I remember about Silvano. First off, he was uncomfortably attractive. Second, that he was a really good guy."

Quite the opposite of what I had imagined to be my dad's response, his magnanimousness, his humor, and his graciousness were more than I could bear. I started to cry.

"Come here, sweet girl," he said as he outstretched his arms. I became a toddler again, reaching for the hand that had steadied me my whole life.

"Alexis," he continued, "your mom and I weren't in a good place then. In fact, things were downright shitty between us and had been for a long time. So, we don't have to pretend your mom and I had any kind of fairytale romance or that either of us were perfect. We were at the end of a marriage that had flatlined and no amount of resuscitation was bringing it back. The marriage simply ran out of gas and I guess I wasn't much interested in the effort to try and save it. We both knew it," he said. Even thirty-five years after their divorce, he was protecting her. I could feel it.

Then he took a deep breath. "But *I* actually have a confession . . ." he said with a timidity that caught me off-guard. He continued. "The truth is . . . I have always known you were not mine . . . biologically."

I was so confused. I thought I was sharing news that was going to absolutely break his heart and he was the one throwing a confession curveball?

"Wait . . . what? You've always known?" I repeated it as though it might help it sink in. "But Mom asked me not to tell you?" I said, thoroughly confused.

"No, she never knew I knew," he said with a smirk. "I did the math and it didn't add up. Your mom and I were basically separated, living together but not sleeping together, so I had a hunch you may not have been mine when she got pregnant." I gaped in astonishment.

"Like I said, our marriage was over and even though she was pregnant, we still filed for divorce. Also, not being a hundred percent sure, of course I was at the hospital when you were born. When I saw your black hair, I whispered to your mom so the nurse couldn't hear, 'Claudia, is she mine?' and your mom looked down without answering as the nurse handed you to me. I knew then and there you weren't my daughter biologically. But then you snuggled into my arms and I looked into your big beautiful eyes . . . and I *chose* you, sweet girl. I chose to be your dad. It is not blood that determines fatherhood or parenthood for that matter. It is love. And love is not a fickle feeling, it's a choice and a relentless commitment. I chose to be all in and never looked back. From that day forward and until my last breath, I still choose you and will continue to choose you. You are my girl . . . and that is the only thing you need to know."

By now I was hysterically crying. Even with the pain of all his broken, healing bones, he reached up and put his hands on my shoulders to try to help me hold it together. More than anything, I was overwhelmed with a profound sense of gratitude. To be the recipient of *that* kind of love, the kind of love not born out of obligation, but voluntary choice from a man who *chose* to love me when he didn't have to.

"Don't get me wrong, I didn't know *who* your biological father was. . . . All this time it was Silvano," he said as he smiled and shook his head. He looked happy to have closed the case on a thirty-five-year-old mystery.

When I finally left, it felt like the ton of bricks that had been on my shoulders had disappeared. I was drunk with relief. I drove to my mom's house to tell her in person about my conversation.

"Wait, he's always known? Oh my God, Alexis. All this time, he knew and he still . . . he chose to be there for you. Oh my God, Alexis," she said as she stumbled backward so that the pantry door could support her weakening knees. She closed her eyes and then slowly slid down the door until she was sitting on the kitchen floor. I could tell that any failings my dad had as a husband—and there were plenty—were forgiven with the same grace he had clearly offered her.

I'd later found out that the weight of this secret was equally heavy for both my parents. My stepmom, Jane, told me that for as long as she'd known me, she had watched my dad struggle with it. Apparently, my dad had played out every possible scenario of how I might find out the truth and was petrified that if or when I did, I'd be angry and blame him or my mom for lying to me all these years. Jane said her vote was always to tell me the truth, but this was a Claudia/Mark decision, so she sat on the sidelines as a silent, supportive teammate.

A few weeks later, the cat was fully out of the bag, my dad was released from the rehabilitation hospital, and we gathered for one of our usual family dinners at my mom's house. This was the first time my mom and dad were seeing each other in person since the big family secret was revealed. My brothers and I secretly shot each other uncomfortable glances and poured big glasses of wine as my stepmom joined us all in the living room for small talk to give my dad and mom a minute alone in the kitchen.

My mom pretended to be busy opening and closing random cabinets as my dad beelined for her. Staring down at the ground and fidgeting with her hands, my mom started, "Mark, I'm just . . . so . . . sorr—" But he cut her off.

"Claudia, we aren't going to do this . . . we aren't going to pretend like there is anything you need to be sorry for. . . . You gave me the greatest treasure of my life. I will always be grateful for that."

My mom had tears in her eyes but was speechless. He took that moment to awkwardly hug her, turn on his heels, and loudly ask, "So what are we having for dinner?"

There was no lightning, no thunder, no angels singing; those of us in the living room all pretended we weren't listening to their not-so-private conversation and quickly went back to whatever we were doing, making it more obvious that we were all eavesdropping. My incredible stepmom walked over to hug my dad and my mom, as relieved as them that this secret no longer needed tending to. Then, per our custom, everyone got in line, grabbed a plate of food from the buffet, and went back to being the loud, sarcastic, loving family we had been before the bomb of my paternity had dropped. My mom thought she would break my heart and my dad's heart. My dad thought he'd break my heart. And I thought I'd break his. Maybe hearts are like bones after all; maybe when they break, they do heal stronger.

CHAPTER FOURTEEN

More than a week after we'd had dinner with my Austin-native-turned-Montanan high school friend Harry, I still couldn't let go of the two big questions he prompted me to pose: *Was the life I had the life I actually wanted? And if not, was I willing to risk everything for what I did want?* I was therefore happy to be in Bozeman, Montana, where I would get a chance to visit with two dear female friends, Carin and Elizabeth. I hoped that time with them might help me find some answers.

I'd met Carin in Los Angeles and she and I had lived there together fifteen years earlier. She is one of those people who has chosen to show up *fully* in this world, both as herself and as an advocate for others on their own journeys. She thinks critically about the cultural pressures and passed-down scripts we unconsciously absorb and read from; she asks the hard questions, challenges the status quo, and defiantly lives as herself in a world with infinite pressure to be like everyone else. A badass single mom, Carin is small, strong, and known for her brutal honesty.

She's like a missile that navigates through your spirit with precision and lands bull's-eyes on the tender parts of you, the ones you thought you could hide from her.

Elizabeth and I met at a TED conference in Vancouver; we had mutual friends, but our own friendship was instant and grew deep quickly. She grew up in Montana, had recently moved back, and was at an inflection point in her marriage. She has big blue eyes, deep dimples, and can pull off a braless sundress like no one I've ever seen. She's airy and feminine; her eyelashes bat at half the speed of a normal human's, so you can't help but feel calm in her presence. She also breathes fire. Like Carin, there is a ferocity to her truth-telling that is perfectly balanced with a graceful fragility and thoughtfulness.

The last few weeks on the road, I'd had a lot of *dude* time. I didn't realize how much I missed being around girlfriends, until—after long hugs—we unfolded our camp chairs and started to talk like old times.

"Hey girl," Carin said nonchalantly, "you lost a pregnancy. Fucking brutal. How do you feel?" She tilted her head back and took a long draw from the cigarette she had just rolled.

"I know life is unfair, we all know that. But it seems like everyone I know is getting pregnant, even those who aren't trying! It's hard to watch people get something I want so badly, and to have it come so easily. It's like I'm drinking this poisonous cocktail of envy, powerlessness, rage, and resentment all mixed into one," I said, knowing I was safe to say anything here, and not be judged.

Carin put her hand on my leg as Elizabeth reached for my

shoulder. "Yeah, it fucking sucks," they said, almost in unison, which made us all laugh.

"I guess the truth is, I'm just feeling really sad and hopeless about wanting something that I have *no control* over. And it feels especially scary that I might never get it . . . and . . . well . . . Brad didn't sign up for this, so . . . I mean . . . I'd understand if, you know . . . if he left me," I said, unburdening myself of the vulnerable truth that I hadn't allowed myself to say aloud to anyone for fear it might come true. They nodded and both leaned in to hug me, validating my sadness and fear.

And we were off. Within minutes, we were sharing the deepest, truest, most painful and most wonderful parts of our lives. Our stories were dipping, diving, and dovetailing; seemingly tying invisible strings as if a holy spiderweb was being woven around us. I was teleported back to the magic of that first I AM THAT GIRL meeting with just six girls, all of us vulnerably sharing and supporting one another.

When I commented on the radiance of our little sisterhood, Carin and Elizabeth mentioned that they were part of a women's group that met weekly to do deep, internal work in a supportive group setting. They described it as a sacred circle of women, a safe place to explore all the feelings that accompanied personal growth, where they'd been given the tools to better love and take care of themselves in the process.

I could feel the impact this group had had on their respective lives. It seemed like there was this whole other invisible world they were now attuned to, a frequency they could hear that was just beyond my ability to register. They had cultivated a deep, knowing self-trust and self-love practice. I wanted more of that. Short of moving to Bozeman to join their women's group— which Carin actually suggested I should do—they insisted I attend an event hosted by the leader, Stacey, taking place in a few days. Both of them would be out of town so couldn't join me, but they thought I'd find it really helpful.

This "event" was a traditional Lakota sweat, which I later googled for context. I read that I could expect to be in a large, dark dome, that it would feel like an oven, and there would be singing and drumming. I also discovered that the Lakota term for sweat lodge was *inipi*, which, translated more directly, means "to live again." I figured that was precisely what I was trying to do, so I texted Stacey and told her that I'd love to join.

On my first day of kindergarten, I wore my hair in long pigtails and I carried a huge, brightly colored backpack that was nearly as big as me. My mom says that it was as though I sensed her nervousness as we pulled into the school parking lot. Apparently, I turned to her and said, "Don't worry, Momma. You're going to be okay. Hope you have a great day." I then puckered my little-girl lips for a kiss, undid my seat belt, and hopped out of the car as if I'd done my first day of school a hundred times before. There were no tears, no looking back, just a brisk walk in the direction of the exciting unknown.

I needed that brave little girl when I got to Stacey's house; now the unknown categorically terrified me. In her midfifties, beautiful, thin, with dark hair and lots of tattoos, Stacey greeted me with a firm, long hug. We promptly climbed into her car and drove together to the "sweat" and to join the company of about twenty other women.

Before being led in the inipi tradition by a member of the Lakota tribe, we stood in a circle and introduced ourselves. I was trying to be present but was distracted by the magnificent backdrop, something right out of *The Lord of the Rings*. In every direction, I was surrounded by the most surreal mountain landscape. The aspen trees were neon green, with leaves fluttering like gold in the sunlight. The air smelled sweet. I could hear a gurgling brook in the background that I came to find was a natural spring you could drink from.

Stacey asked each of us to share something by way of introduction: why we were there, what we wanted to let go of, and what we wanted to heal. When it was my turn, I felt shy and self-conscious, the new girl. Looking down at my feet, I began with the facts.

"Hi, I'm Lex. I'm a friend of Carin and Elizabeth and they told me to come here even though they obviously couldn't make it. I mean, I wanted to come, but they are why I'm here." My nerves were getting the better of me.

"Anyhow, my husband and I . . . umm . . . recently . . . lost a baby—so yeah, I guess that's why I'm here." I could feel the tears welling up in my eyes. Up until this point, I had barely said those words aloud to *my people,* and now here I was announcing them to strangers. The vulnerability burned so intensely that I retreated.

"But it's all good, I mean, I'm good, so . . ." I looked at the woman next to me, hoping she might take her turn and alleviate my discomfort.

"Oh, Mama," Stacey said, "we don't do that here. . . . We don't pretend to be fine when we aren't. Instead, you get to show up exactly as you are. So, thank you . . . what you just shared is big and brave, honey."

Then silence. I kept staring down at my feet, futilely trying to keep my tears at bay. I was now actively praying that the next woman would save me by taking the proverbial mic, but no one said a thing.

Finally, I looked up. To my surprise, Stacey was just looking at me with tears streaming down her cheeks, mirroring mine. Then I glanced around the circle. All the other women were also crying. No one said a word, but just stood there—some with their hands over their hearts as though experiencing my heart-break—in compassionate solidarity.

"Let's all put our hands on our sister," Stacey said to the group, and the group moved in to tightly surround me, hugging me, holding me, laying hands on me all quietly muttering, "Oh sister, honey, darling . . . we love you, we love you so much."

Before I knew it, the dam broke and I was a weeping mess. I fell to my knees on cold earth in a foreign place, as women I didn't know held together all the broken pieces I was too tired to carry alone. And yet more than the frigid ground, I remember the warmth of all the hands and arms and heads covering every exposed part of me. My mouth was wide open, in a silent scream an inch above the earth.

And yet in the midst of my anguish, I was witnessing the raw power of sisterhood, the power of circles, the power of humans laying down their lives for one another, offering to help carry the weight of our collective sorrow. I could feel these strangers offering me a strength I could not muster myself, a faith I had shamefully relinquished, and a hope that felt too dangerous to hold any longer. My heartbreak was certainly present—she would stay with me on and off for some time—but I could simultaneously see another bright spark in the darkness, emanating from their love.

Eventually I regained some composure. I wiped my tears with my dirty hands and stood back up. I reached for the hands of both women on either side of me, rejoining the circle, and allowing other women to contribute their intentions.

We would eventually crawl into that dark inipi together, in and out, four times over a few hours, as was tradition. Each time we crawled out of the inipi, I would make my way to the freezing brook and lie down in the water. With the others I cried, screamed, drummed, wept, swayed, and sweat in the darkness of that sanctuary, praying for our collective healing. With every drop of sweat, I visualized all the control, expectations, insecurities, fears, and sadness rolling off and down my body, being absorbed by the cold earth. I imagined if the ground could speak, she was saying something like, "You keep the love and the hope, darling, but the grief, the hurt, the pain, the people pleasing, all that no longer serves you, is mine."

A year before our RV trip, I went to a promotional event for the famous American soccer player Abby Wambach, who was in Austin to promote her then-new book, *Wolfpack*. During her event she read a few passages, and one in particular gave me goosebumps:

There is a wolf inside of every woman. Her wolf is who she was made to be before the world told her who to be. Her wolf is her talent, her power, her dreams, her voice, her curiosity, her courage, her dignity, her choices—her truest identity . . . Life is harder as a lone wolf. We all need a pack.

At home later, I flipped through her book to find that passage again. I furiously highlighted it and underlined it with lots of asterisks. And in the margin of the book I wrote, "I have people. I have Frannie and a handful of best friends in various cities around the country, but I don't have that . . ." I finished the statement in all caps accentuating this profound epiphany: "I DON'T HAVE A WOLF PACK."

The closest thing I had to a wolf pack was probably my tribe when I was a contestant on *Survivor*. On that small island, hungry and beyond homesick, these people quickly became like family. We looked out for one another, even during the toughest of competitions. A month into the show, my tribe was on a losing streak, and we hadn't eaten a proper meal in weeks. My closest friend, Natalie, was growing thinner and thinner and it was hard to watch her suffer.

On day thirty-one I pulled aside my fellow contestant Erik and shared a plan I'd devised to steal food from the production tent. "I can't watch Nat get any skinnier. She's not okay," I said as he nodded in agreement.

That night we navigated our way through the jungle to the production tent by the light of the moon. When we got there, the local security guard was asleep, so we tiptoed into the tent and foraged for bread, peanut butter, beef jerky, and granola bars that were stacked inside. We were almost out of there when I dropped a jar of peanut butter.

The guard's eyes fluttered open and he took in the two frozen people standing in front of him each with a knapsack full of food. We sprinted outside and ran for what felt like our actual lives. I slipped on rocks and sustained a horrible bone contusion on my left knee, leaving me unable to properly walk for the rest of my time on the island.

The guard pursued us—his flashlight beam darted above and around us as we hid in the jungle—but we eventually made our way back to our shelter, and together, we sat around with dirty hands and filled bellies, laughing at the absurdity of it all.

What Carin and Elizabeth were talking about in this community was the same ride-or-die friendships I'd made on that island. It was a female collective who had each other's backs, and who made a significant commitment to the work, the *real work* of deeply understanding our unique soul's mission. These women were intentionally choosing curiosity over judgment; to letting go of what no longer served them; to setting and maintaining respectful boundaries; to choosing clarity as a form of kindness, self-care as a ritual and personal responsibility; and to providing space for the inevitable oscillation of coming together and falling apart, the death and rebirth of all the versions of themselves.

Stacey was the leader, therapist, counselor, spiritual guide, teacher, Goddess Wrangler, but these women were showing up for each other and themselves, intentionally. Every single week, holding space for one another.

I can now see that my urge to fix and solve problems for other people came from a sincere place of wanting to console others; it also selfishly came out of wanting to assuage and expedite my own discomfort with the uncomfortable emotions *they* were experiencing. It would be a long road of learning to sit with every iteration of my own feelings comfortably before I could offer someone the same grace.

I couldn't help but laugh at the irony of my creating a women's group for others with I AM THAT GIRL long before I knew it's exactly what *I* would eventually need most in my own life.

A few days later, I'd be introduced to more badass women from the group and their husbands and partners. These people weren't just doing brunch, they were doing *life*—together. Theirs was a decision, a commitment, a willingness to voluntarily witness each other's lives, playing together in the sunshine and sitting together in the darkness without trying to fix, heal, or drag one another back into the light.

What, I wondered, would this kind of community have meant to my Grandma Pat? Instead of electric shock therapy, what if she had a circle of women loving her back to life after her many stillbirths? What kind of difference would this have made in my mom's life, if as a single mom, she had felt like there was an entire sisterhood who had her back? How many women and men were going through life bearing the weight of their world on their shoulders, not knowing that our lives are meant to be shared?

The Native American tradition of sweat lodges is both for healing and purification. I felt like that sweat was the starting line of tangibly letting go—not just of our miscarriage but all the broken parts of me I'd been storing in the attic of my mind, thinking if I couldn't see them, they didn't exist. This was the beginning of me letting go of the life I was living for everyone else but me. By the time I returned to our RV, I was like a towel that had been thoroughly rung out: salty, damp, and done for the day. I waved at the boys and went straight to bed. As I fell asleep, I realized that for once, it felt like I had access to a life I didn't want to escape, with people I wanted to learn from and grow, fall apart, and rebuild with. Finally, I had found my wolf pack. Great. But they lived in Montana. And I lived in Texas. So, what the hell was I supposed to do about that?

CHAPTER FIFTEEN

A few weepy good-byes later and we were back on the road. Our time in Bozeman had been a tease. I felt as if the town and that sacred community held the key to my future growth, all the learnings and teachings that I so desperately needed. But as much as I wanted to extend our stay, I had already made plans to see my good friend Kate, who lived a few hours away in Jackson Hole, Wyoming.

As we drove up and over the last Teton peak on our path, we could see Jackson Hole perfectly cradled by the mountains far below and I let out a small gasp. The sun was twinkling off buildings in the distance, the sky was a deep blue, and the valleys looked like they were covered in plush green carpet. Every time I thought the landscape couldn't get any more stunning, it did.

Brad and Luke had planned an all-day guided fishing trip for the next morning, and Kate and I would be going for an "easy to moderate" hike. That said, there's nothing easy or moderate about a hike when high altitude is involved. I did everything in my power to hide the big gasps of air I was sucking in, while Kate continued, nonchalantly chatting away, clearly unaffected by the elephant sitting on my chest.

Kate was different from most of the girls I knew growing up; she defiantly beat to the rhythm of her own drum. It was no surprise that as an adult she would eventually forge her own, unique life path, finding and building a home and a tailor-made life in the dreamy mountains of Wyoming. She spent most of her twenties working at an adventure cycling company called Backroads, leading bike tours through some of the most gorgeous places in the country, and then she eventually settled just outside of Jackson Hole.

While I panted, Kate shared.

"Yeah, I loved working at Backroads, but I was also ready for a change. It's hard to maintain a relationship when you're traveling all the time. I was ready to put some roots down and this was about the prettiest place I'd ever been, so why not, right?" she said in the same casual way Harry had described his decision to also "color outside the lines."

Most of our friends found themselves either never leaving Austin or eventually moving back there. Kate and Harry were anomalies.

"Honestly, I'm not surprised," I said as I stopped for a much-needed water break.

"By what?" she said, not even winded.

"Just that you never settled or fit yourself into some mold of what everyone else was doing. You know—the go to college, get married, move back home, have some kids script most people follow. When we were kids, we were so hopeful, optimistic, rebellious, and everything felt infinitely possible. That kind of eagerness and willingness has faded for so many of our friends as we've become adults. But not you, Kate. Your life is inspiring," I said, shaking my head.

"Aww girl, that's sweet. Honestly, I've always felt that way about you too," she said as she picked up the pace.

Our friendship had spanned over thirty years, so it meant a lot to me that she felt she could say the same about me. Because the younger version of me certainly contained all the qualities I now admired and longed for in her. I was now pretty certain that those parts of me weren't lost forever, that maybe I had just forgotten what junk drawer I left them in.

———

After my early-morning jaunt with Kate and with the boys still away on their fishing trip, I grabbed my journal and walked to a local café. I ordered some food and found a cozy spot at a picnic table to think and write. I started jotting down my thoughts, trying to capture the meaningful moments I had been collecting during our most recent adventures. I looked back at some of the entries from before the trip and noticed that most of my sentences started with "I think . . ." By contrast, the entries from the last few weeks started with "I feel . . ." My heart was speaking up, offering her observations and advice, as opposed to my brain always taking the lead.

Growing up, nobody had ever taught me about my rightful sovereignty, or that the permission and authority I had been seeking externally had only ever been mine to grant. I could now see a plotline familiar from watching all my favorite superhero movies: I was born with all the power I ever needed— I simply didn't know I possessed it, nor how to properly wield it. Being a glutton for comic books, I knew that a superhero's superpowers were almost always revealed on the other side of tragedies, misfortunes, heartbreaks, and devastating loss . . . inevitably around one's darkest moment. So, it actually made sense that all this internal inquiry, struggle, and growth was happening. The ultimate superpower—self-love—was being revealed and I was just now learning how to activate it.

I understood that our Creator was not somewhere out there, above us, looking down, but that the Divine lived and existed inside of us and was us—my father had instilled that belief in me. And yet somehow over the years I had managed to lose contact with the Divine inside of me; I had stopped responding to Her calls, texts, and emails.

As I sat there in the speckled shade of a towering aspen tree, I knew this journey of self-love and radical enough-ness was just beginning, a sacred pilgrimage that would require a daily, spiritual commitment.

And so, as I sat on that little patio in Jackson Hole, Wyoming, I offered my inner voice the floor. I wanted to write in my journal from that place of love and truth that I seemed to understand so well in theory. Only as soon as I put my pen to the paper, I couldn't seem to think of a single thing to write. Frustrated, I took a deep breath and exhaled loudly.

Suddenly I became aware of an older gentleman sitting nearby. He looked very much like the quintessential cowboy actor, with thick white hair, bushy mustache, and sky blue eyes.

Laughing a little as he caught my eye, he said, "Oh yeah, it's really that bad, huh?"

I smiled, a little embarrassed. "Wow, I guess so!" I welcomed the distraction; for a moment the conflict between my head and heart was silenced.

"Anything I can help with?" he said as he scooted a foot closer to me on the community table we were apparently sharing.

"It's just I saw you reading your book and then *trying* to write with an uncomfortable fury, like you were trying to figure out all of life's answers right here and right now," he said knowingly.

"Funny you should say that, actually. Yeah, I feel like I'm at a crossroads in my life and it's a bit scary." Immediately feeling self-conscious that this stranger might think I was looking for some free therapy, I returned to acceptable, superficial niceties. "But hey, we're all just trying to figure it out, right? It will all work out."

"Naw, I don't think it always works out, at least not the way we want it to, or thought it should, ya know?" he said without skipping a beat. *Shit*, I thought, *this guy is down for real talk.*

"So whatcha got?" he said, "Nothing like a stranger to offer unsolicited advice during a deeply significant and personal moment in your life, right?" He grinned.

I figured what the hell, maybe he was a little angel disguised in a sweet grandpa costume.

"Well . . . my husband and I had a big heartbreak and we decided to go on this RV trip—which is why I'm here, with our best friend—well . . . maybe to *heal*, I guess. But now I'm afraid all this 'healing' is *changing* me and changing the things I always thought I wanted. For instance, I think I'm falling in love with the mountains, but we live in Texas. And I finally found this incredible community, but they all live in Bozeman. And we can't just move to Montana. That would be *crazy*. I'm really trying to listen more to my inner voice. But I'm also scared to hear what she might say. It's daunting to make changes to my life but maybe more daunting to *not*, and then have everything go back to how it was. . . . Anyway . . . sorry, that was a lot . . ." I started to trail off and look down at my hands, realizing I'd probably overshared.

"I completely understand," he volleyed back.

I looked up, a little surprised at his attentiveness.

"You do?"

"Sure. I spent a lot of my life knowing something needed changing—often that something was me—but I was too scared to actually do anything about it. So, I just stayed stuck in the abyss of doing nothing . . . and wasting so much time," he lamented.

"If you don't mind me asking, what changed for you?" I asked, secretly wishing I was later going to find out he was some world-renowned psychic and he'd been sent to me to pull some cosmic truth down from the heavens as a divine offering.

"Well, I realized I was just going to keep procrastinating on making any decisions in my life and never really live, as long as I was looking to someone other than me to tell me who I should be and what I should do."

I sighed a little at the simplicity of his statement.

"The real you underneath all that noise always knows the next step. Not the you who you think everyone else wants you to be. And there will come a moment, when being true to who you are becomes the only available option. Because there will always be a dozen voices and twice as many opinions in your life like me, offering unsolicited advice," his said with a smile.

"But the only one that really matters is yours. Loving who you want to love, living where you want to live, and being who you want to be . . . it takes a lot of courage to be who you really are; and even more to know what you really want and to have the guts to go out there into the world and fight for it."

Who was this spirit-channeling, human-whispering, fly-fishing cowboy? And where did this wisdom come from? I was silent for a moment, a little awestruck that he had nailed it, given me the precise advice I didn't even know I needed. He took the pause in the conversation to excuse himself. "Well, thank you for the dance," he said as he started unfolding himself from the picnic bench.

"Umm . . . wow. Thank you, sir," knowing that those two words didn't exactly capture my gratitude.

"Any time, fellow Seeker, anytime," he said as he waved good-bye with his old cowboy hat. I watched as he turned the corner and just like that, he was gone.

After some more reflection, I wrote the following passage in my journal:

It takes a lot of courage to be who you really are; and even more to know what you really want and to have the guts to go out there into the world and fight for it.

All easier said than done.

CHAPTER SIXTEEN

I walked back to the RV and arrived just as the boys were returning from their fishing trip. Luke quickly headed back out to get dinner for us all. Brad asked how my day was as he kissed me. He smelled like sweat, fish, and sunblock.

"It was . . . umm . . ." I searched for the right words.

"Whoa, Lex not able to speak, that's a first . . . this must be good," Brad said, sarcastically but lovingly.

"I actually am . . . a little at a loss for words—and trust me, it's freaking me out too. I just feel like so much is changing and growing and evolving inside of me; my thoughts and feelings actually seem a bit unfamiliar to me. I'm trying to make sense of it all, myself.

"I can't really explain it, but I want more of this . . . whatever *this* is. More aliveness, more remembering who I was before I cared what everyone else thought about me, more swimming in the Yellowstone River, more hiking in these breathtaking mountains . . . more of the things that bring me actual *joy*. . . .

And," I said, gaining momentum, "if we're all working from home anyway . . . I think after we return home from this trip, we should rent an Airbnb in Bozeman . . . maybe just for the summer."

Brad's voice grew low. He looked confused. "Lex, we are not moving to Montana. That doesn't make any sense. I'm sure you can visit, though. I know you love those girls," he said a little condescendingly.

I could feel my voice and my body temperature beginning to rise despite my attempt to keep things at a simmer. "Umm . . . excuse me? What do you mean we aren't moving there and you're sure I can *visit*. Thank you for letting me know where I'm allowed to travel.

"We haven't even talked about it, so how do *we* know if *we* want to move there or not? We make decisions *together*, right? You don't make them for me. *You* don't make them for *us*, am I right?" I barked.

"Babe, don't get me wrong, it's beautiful. But seriously, we are *never* living in Montana, that's just not realistic. So it's cute, but come on."

Now, here's the thing: Brad knows me, really, really, well. Therefore, he knows the passcode to launch the nukes inside me: four little letters, C-U-T-E. I watched his eyes grow to the size of saucers as he realized he hadn't just stepped over the line but had leapfrogged over it; the volcano that he thought might remain dormant was gonna blow.

My eyes became steely, my hands started to shake, but I kept my voice even and quiet—another sign to Brad that shit was about to get real.

"When we started dating, we agreed that you'd play professional basketball for two to four more years and when you retired, the trade-off was that you would move anywhere I wanted to move. So I flew back and forth for years, moving to Spain, Germany, and Turkey with you to make *us* work, because you couldn't travel to come see me during your ten-month basketball season," I said, pausing to look for confirmation from him.

"Okay . . ." he said, trying to anticipate where this conversation was heading.

"Then I took an enormous hit financially, making less than a fourth of what I was making to be able to live abroad with you. I left my company in LA, all of my friends, my professional network, my entire adult life to get on *your* train because you promised me that you'd board *my* train when we were done prioritizing your life and your career."

"Umm-hmm," he said. It was starting to sink in.

"Only, when you retired and I was ready to move back to LA, where I was thriving and where all my professional contacts were, you said we actually couldn't move there because it would be 'too difficult' for you to transition into a new career. You said with you not knowing that many people in LA, we needed to move back to Austin where you would be more 'comfortable.'"(Yes, I was dramatically including air quotes.)

"Only I told you that I wasn't ready to move back to our hometown. And you just shrugged it off and said that's what *you* needed to do to 'provide for us,' even though we both knew I'd be the breadwinner for the next several years while you transitioned into a new profession." His eyes began to squint, which happens when what I'm saying is starting to make sense and he doesn't necessarily want to hear it.

"No . . . I don't think so," he interrupted me. "I don't think that's right. I thought we moved back to Austin because *we* wanted to be there, and it was the best choice for both of us. It's where our family is, and you love it there," he said, trying to convince me of a revisionist history.

But he was right about a lot of it. Almost all of our family lived in Austin. We had just spent a year designing our dream house and were about to start construction on it. Brad had recently joined a new commercial real estate company as a partner, had equity in the company, a team to manage, and a company to build. Although Covid had suspended all my speaking and political aspirations, there was no doubt it awaited me upon my return *if* that was still what I wanted.

We were looking down the barrel of the next thirty years of our lives, overwhelmed by the gratitude of opportunities, financial stability, established community, and all the free babysitting we could imagine when we finally had children of our own. Nothing about leaving Austin "made sense," it was downright *crazy*; but for the first time in my life, I was considering whether the incredible life we *had* was in fact the life I actually *wanted*.

My eyes welled up with rageful tears but they were not directed at him. I was suddenly furious with myself. I had chosen *his* needs, *his* comfort, and *his* security over my own. I hadn't held him accountable—lovingly or otherwise—to our agreement. And I let him think all this time that what he wanted and loved is what I wanted and loved.

This was my pattern. I could see it clear as day now: my willingness to abandon myself, denying my own wants and needs to accommodate and prioritize the wants and needs of someone else. . . all in the name of "love." Brad didn't ask this of me. In fact, he hadn't done anything wrong. We had always agreed that it is his job to communicate his wants and needs; it's my job to communicate mine. And when or if those desires don't align, it's *our* job to find a creative solution. Only I hadn't been communicating any of mine. I had capitulated without him ever asking me to. Like so many women I know, I had, of my own volition, swallowed my wants and desires, muted and diminished myself to ensure my needs weren't an inconvenience for someone else.

For the first time in my life, I could see the value in righteous indignation and sacred rage. Anger was not something I had to fear, control, or shove down; anger was the alarm going off to an invisible fence alerting me that someone had crossed a boundary, even if that someone was me. All this time I had been bypassing my anger, I had been ignoring my soul's inner knowing, dismantling my spirit's built-in security system. I had been denying the very voice advocating for me and trying to protect me.

I could see now that my mom's fury growing up was not about a woman who simply binge drank from time to time, even if it did provide the liquid permission required to tell the truth; it was a warranted, righteous, and sacred response to the years of abuse and trauma she had endured. In a culture that told her to keep her chin up, that she was "fine" and to move on; her unprocessed and unreleased rage *was* sacred, holy even, when I thought about it. It was her spirit communicating that none of the horrific things she endured were okay, and even if it had been years, she was in fact not fine.

Of course, not having the tools to properly process her trauma much less heal it, she, like so many women, attempted to control her anger until she simply was unable to accept the slow death of accommodating others' comfort at the expense of her own. And unintentionally she had modeled that same accommodation to me. Women especially are spoon-fed a version of love that looks like nurturing, saving, rescuing, extending endless second chances, and abandoning our own needs for the sake of others. When in truth, love can also look like firm boundaries, strong accountability, a "go fuck yourself" even, or choosing to love someone from afar because they are too toxic to love up close. We aren't taught to honor our anger because it has something important to share. This was the first time in my life I was actually considering listening to the part of me I had always silenced in the past.

At the same time I was experiencing this holy rage epiphany, I also recognized how unfair it was to be pitching Brad this enormous curveball. He thought "we" had made all these decisions together and that I was perfectly happy living in Austin because that is undoubtedly what I led him to believe, because I wanted it to be true. It's not that I was fooling him; that was unfair. It was that I was willing to and capable of fooling myself to appease him. All the anger I thought I felt toward him for the years I had been in Austin against my wishes was really toward me, for the abandonment of myself.

"Brad, *we* never decided to move back to Austin. *You* did. And I followed you there because I was and am madly in love with you. And at the time, I loved you more than I loved myself. Honestly, I was just so astonished and grateful that I had found someone who adored me so much, who treated me so well, that I didn't want to say or do anything to jeopardize that. So, I agreed to follow you to yet *another* city I wouldn't have chosen for myself. Only it's been eight years that I have prioritized you and what you want, at the expense of myself . . . so when is it my turn, baby?" I said, barely above a whisper. "Because my voice, my joy, my life, and what I want is just as important as yours . . . and what I want right now is to be in Bozeman, with you." I had never communicated what I wanted and needed so clearly in my life. My only fear was, what if he didn't want the same thing as me? What then? Who gets to be the tiebreaker in marriage?

———

Before we ever got married, I asked Brad to do some couples' therapy.

"You know, my mom was married a lot. I don't have that many role models of marriages that inspire me, so before we ever commit to doing life together, I'd like to invest in this both together and individually." I figured he'd subscribe to the "If it ain't broke, don't fix it" mentality, so I was fully prepared for pushback and had already assembled a list of persuasive bullets to explain why I thought therapy was important. To my surprise, Brad didn't resist at all.

"Absolutely, babe, makes total sense to me. You already have someone in mind, or do you want help finding us someone?" he said.

He could see the surprise on my face, so with a big grin, he added, "What? You think I'd be one of those guys who is too good for therapy?"

I shrugged. "I guess I didn't know what kind of guy you'd be when it came to this kind of stuff."

"Well, this is how I see it: Coaches make you better, they train you to be bigger, faster, stronger. They improve your game and in return you become a more valuable player. And if your goal is to be at the absolute top of your game, it requires even *more* work. More investment of time, money, and energy. I don't want an ordinary relationship, I don't want a six or even a seven out of ten relationship, Lex, I want an eleven. And I'm willing to work my ass off, hire the right coach, and do whatever work is necessary to make that a reality," he said with that same sexy swagger he had on our first date.

Needless to say, my man loves himself some therapy and when asked, he is shameless about the impact it has had on his life and our relationship over the years. I've overheard him talk-ing with work colleagues and clients and declining a lunch meet-ing because he'd "scheduled a session" with his therapist.

"Are you ever embarrassed to admit you have a therapist, especially with your older male clients who think therapy is the last-ditch effort to save a failing career, life, or marriage?" I asked him once.

"Not at all," he said, almost offended. "I'm proud to admit I need help and that I'm not perfect. If anything, it's opened up a lot of vulnerable conversations with guys who then felt comfortable sharing what's really going on for them. We're human. We all struggle, so what's the point in pretending we don't? I don't buy into the bullshit that as a dude I'm tougher because I'm just unwilling to admit it. I'm not ashamed about wanting to be a stronger communicator, needing tools to feel less anxious, wanting coping mechanisms for my stress, and self-care practices to feel more confident. And I don't feel embarrassed about hiring a therapist to help me with all of that; to help me be a better version of myself, a better business partner, better husband, and eventually a better father? You kidding?! I'm fucking proud of that, babe!"

Now, in the wake of me asking for what I wanted, Brad was quiet for a minute, staring straight ahead. He wasn't offering excuses, explanations, or a defense for anything. It was clear to me that he was drawing on all that good therapy, that he was sincerely trying to process the situation and to really listen to what I was trying to share.

"I don't know exactly what that means for us, honey," he said with brutal honesty.

"I know. I don't either," I said more softly. The eruption was over. We had both waved our white flags. I crawled into his lap.

"I had no idea all this time that you were so unhappy . . . I don't think I wanted to see it because I was so focused on what felt right for me . . . but, I hear you. We had agreed to moving anywhere you wanted when I retired, and I didn't hold up my end of the deal. That wasn't fair to you . . . I'm really, really sorry, Lex."

We both sat there in silence for a bit. Then Brad put his hand gently under my chin and lifted my face so he could look into my eyes. "I mean it, I hear you, honey . . . I really do. As for moving . . . I don't know. There's a lot to think about . . . and I love you . . . more than anything in the entire world. And wherever you are is my home. So . . . we'll figure something out, *together*. I promise." It had been terrifying to ask for what I actually *wanted*. And it felt overwhelming to have that request fully heard and met with such love and grace.

As much as it was a relief that the storm of our argument was passing, it was also strangely exhilarating to realize that I was starting to speak up for myself. I was finally advocating for what I actually wanted—dare I say, speaking my truth.

I guess I'd always thought that adulting—something I took very seriously—required serious sacrifice. It felt weirdly rebellious to simply ask for the things I actually wanted. And honestly, I kind of thought it was an unspoken agreement all adults made at some point. The idea that "growing up" required a resignation of our childhood fantasies: the actor who quits auditioning, the professional athlete who stops training, the new parent who sells their motorcycle, the artist who puts down their brushes, the entrepreneur who gives up on their start-up, the wanderlust who quits traveling. And while it may be sensible and necessary even, it also just felt so devastatingly heartbreaking.

But now I didn't want to forsake my dreams for a lifestyle that was sensible. Now my head and heart wanted to live together. And like Peter Pan who didn't want to leave Neverland, my heart's desires were getting louder; the part of me that didn't want to exchange my stockings for a suit, my thimble for a cell phone, and my ability to fly for a working email.

Back from picking up dinner, Luke knocked on the door and announced himself as he walked up Thor's steps.

"Hey ya'll, you hungry?" he said—and then he stopped. He saw me, a tired, red-eyed, tear-stained woman curled up in her husband's lap.

"You okay, Lex?" he said with a sincere concern.

"Yeah, just a lot of big feelings," I said. Luke started to pull out delicious ramen takeout, setting the table.

"Well, I can't wait to hear all about them, if and when you're ready to share, sister."

I stood up and started to help unpack the food. I smiled as I noticed that he had also stopped to pick up not one but *two* boxes of graham crackers for s'mores. Luke's timing always felt so divine. Without having to explain anything, he just pulled me in and hugged me tight.

CHAPTER SEVENTEEN

Utah's Zion National Park was an absolute *must* on my list of road trip stops; it would be the last one before we headed home. The RV Park we had chosen was right alongside the Virgin River, and the clear, cold water jetted through the red canyons like an Olympic luge ramp. Most of the other campers were soaking up the sun (some with cold beers in hand) while sitting in portable chairs, submerged up to their waists. The heat was intense, so we quickly followed suit and spent a lazy, beery afternoon watching tubers pass by and idly planning the next day's adventure. We had read about a hike in "The Narrows" that we wanted to check out. It would start as a one-mile hike on a dry, beaten path along the river and then the rest of the hike—whatever additional miles we decided to undertake—would actually be *in* the river. We'd read that the water could range from ankle deep to shoulder deep to life-threatening-flood deep, all depending on the season. This time of year, we could expect ankle or waist levels and we were game to venture as far as our feet would take us.

I had first seen the Narrows hike in my favorite travel book, *Wanderlust*. It was one of the many travel and adventure books I had stacked on our coffee table. What caught my attention was the photo of a man hiking shin deep in crystal-clear water with smooth, dusty red and orange colored rock walls—as tall as skyscrapers—on either side of him. It looked like an elaborate water maze; the tall corridors twisted and turned like a snake. I had daydreamed of one day standing in the exact same place as in that photo, touching those same smooth walls.

We had grown accustomed to just showing up in places without reservations or planning and having our version of Disneyland all to ourselves. Zion, however, was packed. There were no cars or electric bikes available—all were already rented—so we had to settle for good ol' mountain bikes to get us to the hiking trailhead nine miles from our campsite.

The next morning, backpacks loaded with water, sunblock, peanut butter and jelly sandwiches, and snacks, we headed out. The air was chilly and the bike path devoid of other adventurers. The vast landscape seemed untouched by humans and I felt as though I'd been teleported back in time; I half expected to see dinosaurs running nearby, like in a scene from *Jurassic Park*. The red rock wonderland is more than two hundred square miles, and features a beautiful juxtaposition of sheer, deep canyons, lush pockets of vibrant green vegetation, and countless waterfalls.

Not for the first time, I was in awe of the majesty of the

American West. From the stunning night sky in Santa Fe, to the magical pools of Colorado, the big sky and neon green fields of Montana, to the snow-capped mountains of Wyoming, and now, the prehistoric pinks and marbled rock formations in Utah, it all absolutely took my breath away. There was no way to *not* experience awe in the presence of these landscapes. In my mind, they were glittering bursts of bright-colored joy that disrupted the darker, monochromatic canvas that had been my life before the trip. At a loss for words in the presence of that staggering beauty, I kept muttering, "Oh my God."

The initial bike ride was uphill and seemed longer than the advertised nine miles. It left me already out of breath and thinking, *Holy shit, that was just the warm-up?!* We locked up our bikes at the trailhead and followed a handful of other eager early risers onto the dirt path.

When we reached the water a mile in, we stepped into the Narrows and the extreme cold took my breath away. Tilting my head back as far as my neck would allow, I could barely make out the tiny slivers of blue sky above the rock walls. I marveled at the time it must have taken for the water to erode the rock into these magnificent canyons.

I had never hiked through a river, nor had it dawned on me that walking upstream would mean fighting a consistent downstream current. We quickly deduced that the current at the center of the stream was significantly stronger, and so we scurried to the outer edges. This also meant we could each keep one hand on the velvety rock wall, a much-appreciated stabilizer in contrast to the slippery rocks.

For the first hour of our hike, there was a small pack of people in a line behind us. From a bird's view, we must have looked like a class of ants gingerly marching through the canyons on our first day of kindergarten.

About an hour or two in, the current became significantly stronger, and the water grew deeper. Unsurprisingly, many of the hikers behind us decided they'd reached their "thrill" threshold and turned around to head back. Another hour in and anyone who had been walking with us had turned back. Now it was just the three of us trudging along in silence. The only sounds were the ripple of the water and our own splashing as we continued on.

Throughout our hike, I kept thinking back to that *Wanderlust* book. In spite of my savage work schedule, I'd find pockets of time to curl up on my couch and daydream as I leafed through the pages of all the other adventure travel books stacked with it. I looked for the exact spot where I thought the Zion photo might have been taken, wondering if it had been a divine invitation sent for me. I couldn't help but hear Harry's advice to pay attention to the books on your coffee table and think about the way he'd reorganized his life to follow his passion. And Kate's courage to stray from the familiar, grooved path of a more expected life. They'd both given up what they had for what they wanted.

Suddenly I realized that I was standing ankle deep in the same exact place I had seen in my book, my form dwarfed by the smooth red rock cathedral I was walking through.

"Brad!" I yelled enthusiastically. "Please take a photo of me! This is the spot from my *Wanderlust* book!!" Though I had once thought the photo in the book must have been Photoshopped—the red hues *had* to have been enhanced—I could now see that the photo had actually not done this place justice whatsoever. In real life, the setting was exponentially more arresting to the senses and more sublime than *any* photo could possibly capture, mine included.

I walked out into the center of the river, trying to steady myself against the increasing power of the current. I smiled broadly for the camera, and not even the baseball hat shadowing my face could hide my elation.

YES! I thought. *I'm not just daydreaming; I'm actually living this!* I wasn't sitting on my couch fantasizing anymore. I was living the dream of walking in the freezing cold water, through these unearthly, hallowed stone hallways.

The farther we walked, the more demanding our hike became and soon we hadn't seen another hiker for hours. The waters were growing deeper and the currents swifter with every step. At one point the canyon hallway narrowed significantly and a boulder the size of a van blocked the passage, forcing the water around it in two narrow chutes. The ferocity of the current and the size of the roadblock would have made it impenetrable had Brad not turned himself into a human ladder for Luke and me to climb up and over.

As I waded through the deep waters, my mind also navigated through the landscape of my life; the ingrained patterns of thinking I'd grown so accustomed to had unconsciously become my default. My worries, my fears, and my limiting beliefs had become the familiar highways I automatically chose as I settled into the comfortable, responsible, and judicious life I had created. I became more conservative in my willingness to take risks, more obvious in my decision making, and unrecognizably tame. And in doing so, I had simply resigned myself to living a life that no longer resembled my authentic self.

Clearly seeking more thrill, we continued to put one foot in front of the other, oblivious to how far we'd gone or how long we'd been at it. Mesmerized by the idea of what might lie around each next bend, we egged one another on. "Just one more" one of us would shout, pointing to the next switchback of the river. It was as if our childhoods were harkening us back, challenging and daring us to keep going, one step farther, and then another. Maybe, I mused, maybe George Bernard Shaw was right, that we get old because we stop playing, not that we stop playing because we get old. Maybe what really ages us is that we start taking ourselves too seriously, our lives become too precious, and we start caring too much about what other people think. Maybe we become old when we stop chasing spontaneously exhilarating experiences that make us forget to look at our phones and lose track of time.

When I finally looked down at my watch, I was stunned.

"Holy shit, guys," I said loud enough for them to hear me over the noisy water.

"I know we planned on hiking two to three miles in . . . but y'all, I think we've hiked almost ten miles," I said incredulously, realizing that we'd have to retrace every single step to get back home.

Brad and Luke were as shocked as I was. We returned to our senses—and to the pain that each of us was feeling.

For me the cold water had numbed the majority of my body parts. We were often submerged at least up to our waists—and at one point to our chins, forcing us to hold our backpacks high above our heads—I was soaking wet, chilled to the bone. But now, even with the numbness, I knew my feet were in rough shape. I'd made a last-minute decision—now an obvious mistake—to wear a thinner-soled pair of shoes. The next morning, I would barely be able to stand, my feet black and blue from the tip of my big toes to the base of my heels.

Brad finally decided that watching me wince with every step was too much to bear, so he picked me up and carried me for long stretches. We passed several people coming the other way who laughed at the Yeti-sized man carrying a woman—ass in the air—over his shoulder like a Neanderthal who had just chosen his mate.

Thanks to Brad's brute strength, we finally limped back to where we'd left our bikes at the trailhead. We still had the nine-mile bike ride to go, but we took that exceptionally slow; all three of us were starving and exhausted since we had gone through our sandwiches and snacks hours earlier. After we finally arrived at our campsite, we hobbled just a little farther to eat whatever we could find at a small café next to our RV park, then hobbled again back to Thor and set up our chairs in the water—as we'd done when we arrived—soaking up the final sunset of our road trip.

We sat there with our bellies full, exhausted but content.

"I know y'all could stay on the road forever, but I think it's time we head back home," Brad said, interrupting the exhausted silence.

Luke looked at me and winked.

"Come on, buddy . . . two more weeks!"

"Two more weeks! Two more weeks!" I joined in for fun. We all knew that we'd already been on the road weeks longer than Brad had initially agreed to. Two more weeks wasn't gonna happen.

"Nah, I get it, brotha, we gotta go back and face the real world at some point," Luke relented.

For me, this felt like the night before my parents picked me up from summer camp every year. I hated to leave camp. I'd cry in anticipation of already missing everyone and everything. I felt the same sad anticipation welling up inside me now. Our adult summer camp adventure was coming to a close, and I was already dreading returning to "real life."

I leaned my head back, letting the setting sun warm my face before it disappeared behind the Rocky Mountains. We packed up our chairs for the last time from our little watering hole, and we made it back to our RV in time for all three of our exhausted bodies to collapse in our beds for one of the soundest sleeps I had ever had.

CHAPTER EIGHTEEN

The next morning, Brad was like a horse after a long ride, eagerly galloping as soon as he knew he was headed toward the stables. Rather than break up our long ride home over a day or two, he decided he'd rather rip off the Band-Aid and drive straight home without stopping.

"What are you most excited about and most dreading, when it comes to being back home?" I asked. "Luke, you first." He was sitting in the collapsible chair we had set between the two captain chairs on our first day.

"Good question," he said, pausing. "I think I'm excited about forging a path forward and also dreading the path forward," he said. I nodded in agreement.

"Something similar for me," I said vulnerably. "I'm excited to figure out the next steps on the fertility front and I'm also dreading more potential heartbreak, knowing there are no guarantees on the baby front . . . home front . . . work front . . . all fronts, I guess . . ." Brad reached across Luke to grab my hand. "Me too, baby," he said.

Grabbing our hands in his own, Luke got sentimental.

"We started out as the brokenhearted amigos, and while we still have a long way to go, it's hard to believe *this* version of us as we head home," he said, getting all gushy.

"Awww, Luke!!" I said dramatically.

"I'm serious," he said. "I couldn't imagine my life without y'all. These past several weeks have been some of the hardest of my life and some of the best. All our early-morning coffees, hikes, tough love convos . . . there's no one I'd rather be on this wild ride with than you two," he said as we smiled in agreement.

Luke was right. Together, the three of us had helped pick up and reassemble each other's broken pieces. Not fully healed, but well on our way—together, it seemed—we had the collective courage to imagine a brighter future for ourselves.

———

Brad and Luke took turns driving home eighteen hours straight. I however slept soundly through the night and only woke up when I felt the RV come to a stop. I sleepily looked outside to see our white house with its blue door. Brad had texted my mom that we were almost home, so she was sitting in a rocking chair on our front porch, holding our beloved Gussie, whom she had taken care of while we were gone. Gussie jumped from her arms and sprinted to me when we stepped out of Thor. My mom was right behind her. We gladly accepted kisses and hugs from them both.

After we'd unloaded the RV, my mom joined me in my room as I started to make piles of laundry and put away a few clean clothes. We chatted, catching up on the time apart from each other, and I reveled in our renewed closeness. Growing up, my mom was never my "friend." Instead, she made it very clear that she was first and foremost my mother, tasked with the job of protecting me and teaching me to one day fly out of the nest, successfully.

It wasn't until my midtwenties that my mom and I hit the friend zone. I remember the moment things changed. I was at her house, post graduate school, and I noticed that she was just staring at me and smiling. When I couldn't take the awkwardness anymore, I asked her what she was grinning at. She paused, then said, "I'm just realizing that my job here is done. You're all grown up, Alexis. . . . Now I just get to enjoy you." It seemed that she was reveling in that kind of moment again, and I was utterly delighted by her adoration.

After my mom left Brad and me to our unpacking, I stood alone in the entranceway to our bedroom. I held my breath, anticipating the reemergence of my grief and the excruciating body ache I'd had when I was here last. I gritted my teeth and flexed my muscles tightly, bracing for the blow of that old feeling. But there was only silence, stillness.

Feeling a little more confident, I exhaled and then I went into the room and sat down on the edge of the bed. I looked at the nightstand, remembering what was inside. I reached over and ever so gently opened the top drawer. There they were: the baby unicorn slippers. I started to cry, but this time not out of the same kind of bone-deep sadness as before. I wasn't feeling angry or resentful. Instead, I cried out of hopefulness.

I held the slippers to my chest and let out a loud sigh. I knew beyond a shadow of a doubt that I would one day hold a baby in my arms. Someday, somehow.

Over the next several days, I felt so strange and so new in this old life of mine. I've heard it said that true empowerment is the mere recognition that choice exists. Yet there were so many choices, opinions, expectations, assumptions, and agreements I'd made and accepted in my life. Until now I'd never questioned them, much less acknowledged that I was the author, captain, and final decision maker in my life. Our RV trip had planted so many new seeds, so much awareness. All these new observations, questions, and considerations required water, time, and tending to. With fresh eyes and a full heart, I was getting to do the soulful work of reevaluating the life I *had*, and deciding if it was, in fact, the life I *wanted*.

Over the next week Brad and I had a dozen more conversations about my desire to be in Bozeman. Me silencing myself was no longer an option; it was a pattern I had outgrown and discarded like an old sweater that no longer fit. So I made a different choice, and I continued to advocate on behalf of the newly discovered voice inside of me, knowing there was an intuitive reason I was being called to those mountains, to that community, trusting the unknown forces pulling me back there.

Brad could see how important this was to me, how much I needed it, because I was crystal clear with my request. Eventually, he ended one of these conversations about logistics with "As you wish, baby," nodding to one of our favorite films, *The Princess Bride*. "No way!! Really?!? We're doing it?!?"

I suggested that we take baby steps. No major decisions. No major commitments. He agreed to renting an Airbnb for a month, which was an easy sell: to sacrifice steamy, hundred-plus-degree Texas summer weather for the cool, lush mountain life of Montana. Luke was privy to several of my conversations about wanting to go back to Bozeman and had shared a similar desire, so he was my next call.

"Luke!!" I said before he even had a chance to say hello, "Brad's on board for getting a rental for a month in Montana! I told him I'd call and see if you wanted to join?"

Not wanting the three amigos adventure to end, Luke was all in. By virtue of what felt like another mysteriously divine firefly moment, in less than a week I had secured an adorable two-bedroom place that the three of us could share, just south of Main Street, next to a beautiful little park.

When we arrived back in Bozeman, I promptly scheduled regular therapy sessions with Stacey in the colorful yurt behind her house, and I joined the wolf pack women's group that met every Tuesday. Carin and Elizbeth were right. Sitting in that circle of women *was* life changing as I continued the work of learning *how* to better love myself.

Brad initially joined me for couples' therapy, but eventually he found so much personal value in our sessions with Stacey that he started scheduling his own time with her. One of the most profound things she said to us in our first session was, "You can't heal in the same place you got sick." Montana became a new place for us to prioritize our healing, our learning, and our growing as we put into practice all that she was teaching us about ourselves and each other.

With Covid restrictions still in place, I remained unable to travel for work. This allowed me the time to really invest in hiking, heading out onto a new trail each and every day. Sometimes I'd hike with a friend; a lot of the time I went alone. When alone, I'd put in my ear buds and walk until my feet hurt, then I'd walk some more. I'd regularly be so exhausted when I got home that I didn't have the energy to feel anxious about a future I couldn't control or be depressed about a past I couldn't change.

Some days, I hiked with such fury that I'd be panting, out of breath, keeled over wondering if my lungs were going to explode. Other days I was barely able to put one foot in front of the other and wondered if going back to bed was the better choice that day. And some days I did just that: went back to bed.

Then there were days I'd hike until I found a good place to sit or lie down and just cry unapologetically, with no one around to judge me or ask me what was wrong. There were also days that I simply felt blissful. Sometimes I sang loudly to my favorite music; other days I just listened to the birds and the rustling of the animals. Some days I screamed and howled into the wind, savagely flinging my rage into all four cardinal directions and every degree in between. Other days, when I made it to the top of a summit, I would quietly pray and sit in awe of Mother Nature's majesty.

Every day was different. But the commitment was the same, to be outside, to put my feet on the earth, to walk into the mountains, to breathe and to be with God. And every day I communed with Her, I experienced the purest form of my joy, a quiet peace that transcended understanding or circumstance. And every day, one step after another, I grew stronger.

As the weeks went by, I watched the electric green fields sway in the wind, the flowers explode with varying deep hues of color. I witnessed the long summer days, packed with hikers, campers, fishers, and floaters shorten as the jewel-toned landscape was slowly replaced with muted golds and rusted oranges. I felt the warm days cool, eventually turning into a crisp, snow-covered winter wonderland. Yeah, no surprise, we stayed longer than we planned. How could we not?

At the end of the first month, Brad, Luke, and I had a family meeting to discuss staying for "one more month." With the same curiosity and enthusiasm of what might be around the next bend when we had hiked through the Narrows in Zion, we said yes and kept saying yes . . . as the three of us continued straddling two worlds: Austin and Bozeman, two places we loved equally, for completely different reasons.

CHAPTER NINETEEN

When I answered the phone call from a Beaumont area code, I heard the voice of a man that sounded foreign and yet strangely familiar.

"Is Alexis there?" he asked.

"This is her," I said, knowing I sounded too formal.

"Hi, this is Silvano Jr. You sent me a message about my dad on Facebook."

Shortly after the biological fiasco was resolved in my family, my dad pulled me aside. He told me that he thought it was only natural if I had any desire to meet my biological father. I certainly didn't need a new daddy—I had been raised by the best. But I'd be lying if I said I wasn't curious to meet the man who'd given me my brown eyes.

With my dad's blessing, I reached out on social media to the only contact I could find for Silvano Sanchez, his son and my half-brother. I wrote him a private message, claiming that I was helping my mom reconnect with some of her old soccer teammates from forever ago. I said I was hoping to connect with his dad if he was comfortable sharing his contact information with me.

So, I should have somewhat expected this call. But it still felt shocking. I only vaguely remember the details of that first conversation, but I do know that we got beyond my ruse of finding old soccer teammates and Jr. cut to the chase pretty quickly. He had known I might exist somewhere in the world, he said. His parents had divorced decades ago, and his dad had mentioned over the years that he thought he might have a half-sister somewhere. Silvano Sr. had seen me at a soccer game when I was a toddler once and apparently the resemblance was staggering. Jr. was smart and had put it all together when he'd seen my message. That, and the fact that we are the spitting image of each other. Nature don't lie, y'all.

Before he got off the call, Jr. said without my prompting, "By the way, you have a big sister! And we'd love to meet you in person . . . and so would Dad."

A few weeks after that unbelievable phone call, Brad and I drove six hours to a restaurant a mile from where I was conceived to meet my biological father and half-siblings.

Despite his longtime separation, my existence still represented a stain on the fidelity of Silvano's marriage. Yet the first thing he did when he met me was put one hand over his heart and the other over his mouth as he leaned in to hug me and whisper, *"Mi hija"* ("daughter" in Spanish). Overwhelmed, I started crying. Not because I was in need of a dad, and not because he was in need of another daughter. But because yet another human existed in my life who despite the potential shame, guilt, or fear . . . chose love. And that I have been the lucky recipient of that choice and commitment twice over. I also cried for all the painful hours, weeks, and months I had lost sleep over my evolving birth story. I cried for the many years my parents had lost sleep over it, unaware that the other knew the secret. I cried for the cost this secret had on both of their lives as well as the freedom created when it was released.

While there are many ways to define a person's identity—a birth certificate, social security number, race, gender, ethnicity, sexual preference, gender preference, religion, political party—it has become clear to me that the foundation by which I exist rests squarely on a single data point: that like my brother Josh mentioned so many years ago, I am profoundly loved.

Only now I realize that we can only accept love to the extent we love ourselves. Sadly, we can't simply outsource love from others; it requires that we go on a journey to do the hard, deep "heart work" and remember how to radically love ourselves first. My dad was right that parenthood is not about biology, and neither is our wealth about money or the people surrounding us. I am a billionaire in love not because of the broken, failing love I have known or even because of the supernatural, unconditional love I have known; I am a billionaire in love because I have dared to love *myself* that much.

I love Michelangelo's philosophy "Every block of stone has a statue inside it, and it is the task of the sculptor to discover it." He understood that it was his job to simply "Set free the angel captured in the marble." There is a great relief in surrendering to a higher power and simply acknowledging that we are but a vessel *revealing* something, not necessarily the source from where the angel or genius originates.

I wonder if the same applies to our lives. That it's not our job to be eloquent, to offer a formula for re-creating success, keys to achieving happiness or sculpting brilliance. Rather, like Michelangelo, we only need to chisel around and release the beautiful and heartbreaking stories embedded inside our marbled lives. I also wonder if every person like me wonders whether their story is important enough or interesting enough to be shared. Then again, maybe it's just our human nature, trying to feel worthy of sharing the heaven that exists inside each of us.

Because when we do share our sacred stories, not to impress, instruct, or even inspire, we vulnerably and bravely offer another human the purest, most precious gift we have to offer, an authentic and honest piece of ourselves.

However, in our sharing, it feels emotionally irresponsible and reckless to glide over our traumatic experiences, tidying up and shortening the time line, because it sets unrealistic expectations for our fellow seekers on a similar path. It's as if throwing glitter and powdered sugar on our wounds will expedite the process and make the gruesomeness less gruesome. The road to healing and learning *how* to really love ourselves—especially the parts of us we don't like all that much—is often an arduous zigzag, two steps forward, five steps back, that is significantly harder and more time-consuming than any of us wants to admit.

There is no person, no book, no inspirational mantras; nothing that will reduce our pain other than time. Anything claiming otherwise is profiting off our desperation with snake oil and fake Sherpas, pretending to alleviate the burden that is ours and ours alone to carry. Because when we own our heartbreak, when we brand it with our initials and reclaim it, in all its painful, gory glory, we stand at the starting line of a journey that ends with it eventually hurting less.

Grief is often described as being in a cocoon or experiencing a season of wintered hibernation. I love the image that in our most agonizing moments, our instinct is to turn inward and to disappear into the unknown, into the darkness. Looking back, my "wall staring" before we left for our road trip allowed me to disappear into this kind of cocoon. I just didn't know it then. All of me was changing, turning into something else, something new.

The Merriam-Webster dictionary's definition of *apocalypse* is "the end or destruction of the world." I wonder if all of it—finding out the truth about my biological father, a global pandemic steering my career and finances straight into a brick wall, and our losing a baby—was an apocalypse, and if the continued infertility challenges we'd face over that next year were echoes from the initial blast, like aftershock waves leveling whatever was left standing.

Existing as I do now—on the other side of that mushroom cloud—I can't help but wonder if throughout our lives, maybe our worlds are actually *meant* to fall apart, to be destroyed and wash away? Because in the process, it seems we're gifted an invitation to continuously reinvent ourselves; to rebuild something better, something stronger and something truer . . . over and over again. I cannot help but think about how differently my life would look had I stayed on the superhighway I was on, had there not been a divine detour rerouting me.

Witnessing the changing seasons in Montana has changed me—the vibrancy slowly dying, stark winter putting everything and everyone into a state of necessary hibernation, then the warmth returning and the baby seedlings beginning to raise their brave little heads, defiantly hopeful for another opportunity to bloom. Having never lived in a place with four seasons, I am learning from Montana that we, too, have seasons, specific times for things to grow, for things to die, and for things to bloom again.

Maybe I was called to Bozeman because my soul knew that I needed to witness that tangible example of transition so I could let the winter freeze away the old parts of me and patterns that were ready to die: all my people pleasing, attention seeking, and need for external validation. All the while germinating the seeds of self-love and acceptance that would never have opened otherwise, never have taken root and never have grown into the rich garden from which I now write.

Due to the seedlings that were planted inside of me on my RV adventure, all the new ideas, perspectives, practices, and possibilities that didn't previously exist have grown thick, strong roots over these past two years. My internal landscape may have been ravaged by wildfires, but like the spring starting to awaken outside the window from where I type, I too see the first blooms audaciously and bravely breaking through the previously scorched earth.

Every day now, I try to practice many of the rituals I learned on my Joy Hunting adventures as they continue to grow deeper roots and taller branches within me:

I make a point to slow down in order to be present to all the tiny, perfect and imperfect moments that make up the various threads in the tapestry of my life. Operating at a slower pace, I'm able to respond instead of react to life, aiming to accept what is without trying to control it or change it.

I strive to love myself fully and to give permission to the messy, shadowy parts of me to co-exist with all my resplendent parts. I find pretending to be perfect or offering a curated version of myself is not only exhausting, it prevents me from having truly authentic and intimate relationships in my life. Plus, I find I'm far more interesting and far more fun when I'm not pretending that I always have my shit together.

I remind myself that letting go of others' expectations and opinions of me allows my inner voice to be my truest and best guide. I believe that validating myself is the single most powerful act in the pursuit of self-love.

I choose my community—the people I do life with—intentionally. I love infinitely. I trust discerningly. I forgive quickly. I communicate boundaries clearly. And I lovingly let go of people who are incapable or unwilling to give as much as they take.

I take the time to get clear about what I actually want. I then ask for it and if need be, I fight for it.

Being courageous enough to give up the life I had—even if it felt crazy to others—for the life I really wanted was the first step to living the life of my actual dreams.

And last, per my promise to my teenage self, I allow my childlike curiosity to run freely and continue to chase adventures to keep my internal bonfire burning bright. I've always believed that growing up was a trap. So I choose to remain wild.

I set out to the save the whole world, and all I ever really wanted was my own love and respect. And I had to lose everything I thought made me matter, to see that I mattered all along. What teenage Lex had known all those years ago was I never needed any of that other stuff, because I had always been . . . enough. Radically enough. I had just forgotten. My spark had just gone out and I didn't remember what it felt like to live a life that was really *mine*.

This past birthday, I chose to celebrate my Latina heritage and I threw myself a quinceañera birthday party. I was proud to honor the coming of age of the Mexican girl inside of me. Even if my dad and my biological father were not present to officially usher me into this wild world, I invited all my friends and danced with my husband as I ushered *myself* into this next iteration of my life. I even wore a bedazzled pink princess dress with a six-foot-wide petticoat as I might have done at age fifteen. Beyond the sequins and celebration, however, I read about and took to heart the meaning of this rite of passage in a young woman's life.

Then a few months later, the local Bozeman community

theater was putting on *A Christmas Carol*. Despite being utterly terrified and crying in the car on the way to my audition, I mustered up the courage to do it anyway. Because nine-year-old Lex deserved another shot at doing something she once loved, even if some Derek Funderbutt might be waiting in the shadows to ridicule me. I was delighted when I actually got cast because just being part of the production changed the narrative of the story I'd been telling myself, that I'd missed my childhood window to explore acting, singing, and dancing, and that I was too old to start now. I had decided that simply enjoying something was a good enough reason to do it, and I certainly didn't have to be good at something to love doing it. My family flew out from Texas and sat in the front row for my opening show, cheering for me and throwing me flowers on stage as if I were the lead in a Broadway play. I was completely over the moon.

I've often wondered if Heaven is just a hidden dimension in ordinary life, an alternate universe that exists here on Earth. And if so, maybe Joy is the door we walk through to experience it. One foot in the seen world, one foot in the unseen world is how I navigate my life now; living from my head *and* my heart, trusting and believing that there are intangible forces always with my best interests in mind, constantly rerouting me, even and especially when I can't see them or feel them.

For years I have secretly prayed and negotiated with God against the odds, against science, against the opinions of a host of fertility doctors. I have defiantly and unsuccessfully pleaded with the universe to grant me and my husband this one, small favor . . . this still unrealized dream, a baby of our own.

I want it all. I want the stretch marks. I want the sleepless nights and the sore nipples. I even want the fussing and crying and shit-filled diapers. Because I also want the cooing, the first smiles, the first step, and the tiny little person who will one day recognize me, reach for me, and call me Mama.

I wish I could tie this story up with a pretty bow, concluding it as a happy, sleep-deprived mama. As I type, however, our prayers remain unanswered. We're continuing to try, but our path to parenthood remains circuitous and unknown. We have, however, opened every door: trusting that the *how* no longer matters and the *when* will arrive on its own terms. And we choose to believe that one day we will be parents to a child, whom we will love beyond what we thought was possible.

After two years ping-ponging between Texas and Montana, Brad recently got his dream job, just outside of Bozeman. He likes to tell people that I am the reason we came to Montana. And I tell them, he is the reason we stayed.

Only now can I see that with no painful apocalypse, there would have been no road trip. With no road trip, there would be no Montana. With no Montana, there would be no great mountain love in the history books of Brad's and my life story. Sure enough, there was purpose to all of that pain, because that unexpected and unwelcomed detour brought us to this majestic place, with this magnificent community that we now call home. And while "heart work" will always be the hardest work we ever do, it will also be the most rewarding work we ever do.

For the first time in my life, I am okay being in the middle of my very unfinished story. I wasted so much time trying futilely to control the various outcomes of my life, instead of simply accepting and enjoying the unfolding adventure as it is, not as I want it to be. And I've finally accepted that we as human beings were simply not built to *know*; we are built to feel and to experience life.

At some point, I started looking at question marks as problems that needed solving, instead of unanswered surprises and the twists and turns in the road on the wild journey of our lives. So now I choose to sit in the temporary discomfort of my unfilled dreams, okay with not knowing the final score of the game because I know the game is still being played and the story of my life is still being written.

I do, however, know that inevitable heartbreak *and* unrelenting joy both await me in the shadows of the unknowable and uncontrollable future. Because that is the inevitability of this awesome human experience. I also know that we are not defined by what we lose; we are defined by who we love and how big and deep we choose to love them, even and especially on the other side of that inevitable heartbreak. In order to fully see and appreciate the light means we sometimes have to dance in the darkness.

So now, I no longer waste time anxiously preparing, anticipating, bracing, rehearsing, and attempting to control the outcome of my life . . . or *anyone* or *anything*, for that matter. Not because heartbreak and disappointment won't hurt; pain is pain. It always hurts. But because just as in Montana, I now know that the seasons are unavoidable. We all will bloom, burn, wither, die, and eventually blossom and bloom once more.

I've accepted that while I won't always get what I want, when I want it, or how I want it . . . the journey I go on in pursuit of it will *always* be worth it. And that every time I stumble, every time I faceplant, every time I get lost or forget who I really am, Joy will be there as bright fireflies in the dark, divinely sent to guide me back home.

ACKNOWLEDGMENTS

Thank you to the entire dream team of people who helped bring this book to life. In no particular order . . .

My wolf pack: Sara, Elena, Lynds, Lils, Chris & Crystal, Virginia, Nikki, Shan, Bec, Illy, Blake, Yogs, Josh, Ryan, Toni, Susan, and Stacey . . . y'all make me braver than I would ever be alone.

Frannie, you know. Ride or die. Always and forever to infinity and beyond.

Nick, thank you for the divine invitation . . . an RV trip for the history books. You are and will always be our big brother and we love you so much. To so many more adventures to come.

My entire family, I live to make y'all proud and I love you all more than any words could ever do justice. Daddy, thank you for choosing to love me so fiercely. It's because of your radical love that I have always had the audacity to fly. Mom, thank you for being my best friend and the most badass woman and mom I have ever known. I am a billionaire in love because of this family.

Bradley, thank you for co-creating this beautiful life with me here in Montana and for your lifelong commitment to doing the real work—because of which—you continue to be my favorite human in the whole world, my soul mate, the greatest love of my life, and undoubtedly (one day) the best father on the planet.

To the exceptional women on my team: WE DID IT!!! Thank you . . . Michelle for your fierce mentorship over the past two decades, for always believing in my dreams and for bringing me into the CAA family. Mollie for being the most supportive agent and friend, and for doing so much heavy lifting to help secure my dream publisher. Penguin Random House for being my dream publishing house and especially to my dear friend and publisher, Marnie, for saying YES to making this book a reality, for giving me a professional home from which to write, and to all the books yet to be written together. Pam, for being the world's best editor and for becoming my surrogate "auntie" throughout the process. Danielle for being both my best friend and the dreamiest publicist in the world. Taryn for helping me best serve this beautiful online community.

ABOUT THE AUTHOR

Alexis Jones is a speaker, activist, and author of *I Am That Girl*. The recipient of the Jefferson Award for Outstanding Public Service, she has been featured on Oprah's SuperSoul100, AOL's Makers, DELL's Inspire100 list, Fast Company's "Female Trailblazers," ESPN's "Pop Culture's Top Ten," and is a Girl Scouts' Woman of Distinction. With a TEDx Talk that received more than 1 million views, Alexis starred in the ProtectHer documentary and created an educational program for male athletes on the importance of respecting women. She has been invited to speak at the White House, the United Nations, Harvard, Stanford, West Point, the Naval Academy, Nike, Google, Facebook, the NFL, as well as in Division I locker rooms all over the country.

Fun facts: Alexis survived 33 days as a contestant on the hit CBS TV show *Survivor*, has backpacked in more than 50 countries, traversed all seven continents, hiked 150 miles to the base camp of Mt. Everest; she said *yes* on *Say Yes to the Dress*, is an ordained minister, and won the Showcase Showdown on the *Price is Right*.

After falling madly in love with the Bridger mountains, Alexis, her husband (Brad) and their French bulldog (Gussie) now call Bozeman, Montana . . . home, sweet, home.